EISENMAN/
KRIER

EISENMAN/ KRIER: TWO IDEOLOGIES

A CONFERENCE AT THE
YALE SCHOOL OF ARCHITECTURE

THE MONACELLI PRESS

First published in the United States of America in 2004 by
The Monacelli Press, Inc.
902 Broadway
New York, New York 10010

Copyright © 2004 The Monacelli Press, Inc., and
Yale University School of Architecture

All rights reserved under International and Pan-American Copyright Conventions. No part of this book may be reproduced or utilized in any form or by any means, electronic or mechanical, including photocopying, recording, or by any information storage and retrieval system, without permission in writing from the publisher. Inquiries should be sent to The Monacelli Press, Inc.

Library of Congress Cataloging-in-Publication Data
Eisenman-Krier : two ideologies : a conference at the Yale School of Architecture.
p. cm.
Includes bibliographical references.
ISBN 1-58093-139-1
1. Eisenman, Peter, 1932– —Aesthetics—Congresses.
2. Krier, Léon—Aesthetics—Congresses. 3. Architecture, Postmodern—Congresses. 4. Classicism in architecture—Congresses. 5. Deconstructivism (Architecture)—Congresses. I. Yale University. School of Architecture.
NA737.E33E4 2004
720'.9'045—dc22   2004014363

Printed and bound in Italy

Editor: Cynthia Davidson
Designer: David Frisco
Yale School of Architecture Publications Editor:
Nina Rappaport
Editorial Assistant: Hannah Purdy

ILLUSTRATION CREDITS

The Architecture of the Italian Renaissance by Peter Murray (New York: Schocken Books, 1986): 72

© 2004 Artists Rights Society (ARS), New York/VG Bild-Kunst, Bonn: 114 right

Courtesy James Corner Field Operations/Stan Allen Architect: 66

Peter Eisenman Archive; Collection Centre Canadien d'Architecture/Canadian Centre for Architecture, Montreal: 16–17

Dick Frank: 68 top left

Giuseppe Terragni: Transformations, Decompositions, Critiques by Peter Eisenman (New York: The Monacelli Press, 2003): 97

© Archives at the Goetheanum: 114 left

John Jacobson: 132–33

© Musée Granet, Aix-en-Provence, France: 111

© Namuth Photo Ltd.: 121

RIBA Library Photographs Collection: 103, 119

© Sant'Agostino, Rome: 112

© Estate of Robert Smithson; Courtesy James Cohan Gallery, New York/Licensed by VAGA, New York, New York: 84

© Estate of Robert Smithson/Licensed by VAGA, New York, New York: 85

Courtesy Robert Somol: 86

Albert Speer & Partner GmbH: 98, 100, 101

Courtesy Monika Sprueth Gallery/Philomene Magers; © ARS, New York 2004: 77

With permission from the Superstudio archive curator: 82 bottom

Views of Rome Then and Now by Herschel Levit (New York: Dover Publications, 1977): 80

Courtesy Yale University Visual Resources Collection: 123, 127

7   **Foreword** ROBERT A. M. STERN
9   **Between Utopias and Ideologies** JOAN OCKMAN
16 **"Eisenman/Krier: Two Ideologies" Exhibition, Yale School of Architecture, 2002**
21 **Architecture and Ideology** ROGER KIMBALL
31 **Eisenman and Krier: A Conversation**

HISTORY

43 **No** SARAH WHITING
53 **"Colin Rowe"** ANTHONY VIDLER

URBANISM

65 **Figures, Fields, Fragments** STAN ALLEN
79 **A Funny Thing Happened on the Way to the Forum: The Nolli Plan and Other Italian Jobs** R. E. SOMOL

POLITICS

91 **How Eisenman Cut the Gordian Knot of Architecture: Looking at Giuseppe Terragni (1904–1943) from Afar** KURT W. FORSTER
99 **On Albert Speer** MAURICE CULOT

LANGUAGE

111 **Ex Nihilo Nihil** DEMETRI PORPHYRIOS
119 **The Art of Listening to Architecture** MARK WIGLEY

THE ARCHITECTS

135 **The Arcadian, the Utopian, and Junkspace** PETER EISENMAN
139 **Coming to Terms with Janus** LEON KRIER

149 **Afterword** VINCENT SCULLY
154 **Milan Pavilions** PETER EISENMAN AND LEON KRIER

160 **Contributors**

FOREWORD

Robert A. M. Stern

The work of Peter Eisenman and the work of Leon Krier represent two opposing and uncompromising formal and ideological views in architecture—deconstruction and reconstruction. But rather than each simply stating his point of view, as though the other did not exist, Eisenman and Krier have engaged in a continuous debate that has redounded to the great benefit of architecture. Many observers have mistakenly characterized the debate as one without common ground. Such is not the case. Though their built work could not be more different, these two immensely cerebral architects share a commitment to architectural language, to architectural scholarship, and most importantly, to the art and act of building as crucial to culture as a whole. The Eisenman-Krier debate, initiated in the 1970s, continues to challenge us today and, to a remarkable degree, continues to define the boundaries of contemporary architectural thinking.

During the lively and sometimes heated symposium "Eisenman/Krier: Two Ideologies," held at the Yale School of Architecture in November 2002, there was opportunity for historic reckoning and also for serious reflection by scholars from different points of view. The resulting essays, published in this book, consider Eisenman's and Krier's work in relation to issues of historiography, theory, linguistics, and the general culture, issues that are central to the architecture and urbanism of our time. This book will offer an important opportunity to take stock of our heritage from the recent past as well as an opportunity to reconsider the discourse and reality of contemporary architecture as we go forward in a new century.

The symposium coincided with an exhibition of the same name, in which two independently conceived shows, also illustrated here, featured Peter Eisenman's House IV and Leon Krier's Atlantis project. The House IV section was initiated by Phyllis Lambert and organized in association with the Canadian Centre for Architecture, where it was curated by Louis Martin and designed by Peter Fianu. The Atlantis portion was designed by Leon Krier in collaboration with Dean Sakamoto, director of exhibitions at Yale; projects were lent to the school courtesy of Hans-Jurgen and Helga Muller of Stuttgart, Germany.

I wish to thank Cynthia Davidson for editing this book and Nina Rappaport for overseeing it as publications editor for the school. I also wish to thank David Frisco, the book's designer, and Andrea Monfried at The Monacelli Press. The symposium and the book's publication were made possible through the generosity of Enid Storm Dwyer, the Elisha-Bolton Foundation, and Gilbert P. Schafer III (M.Arch. 1988). It is thanks to them that this dialogue will take its proper place in the architectural history and architectural historiography of our time.

Between Utopias and Ideologies

Joan Ockman

Everyone knows how, at an exhibition staged at the Museum of Modern Art in 1932, Philip Johnson and Henry-Russell Hitchcock eviscerated European modern architecture of its social and political content. Their aim was to repackage it for American consumption—to make it, as the housing reformer Catherine Bauer said at the time, "safe for millionaires," or as the architectural historian Colin Rowe would put it later in his introduction to the book *Five Architects*, "safe for capitalism." In the ensuing decades, modern architecture, now widely known as the International Style, and having become an American export rather than a European import, evolved into a mainstream aesthetic in which technological innovation and formal virtuosity trumped the earlier reformist aspirations. A new, Cold War ideology of "the end of ideology"—a slogan popularized by the American sociologist Daniel Bell in a 1960 book of that title—replaced the older Marxist and socialist allegiances while implicitly forwarding the objectives of capitalist modernization. For Rowe, modernist culture's utopian program to bring about a more egalitarian and democratic society had proved illusory and, even worse, had revealed its authoritarian side. The only escape from the evil twins of totalitarian dictatorship and technocratically driven consumer culture now appeared to be architecture as art, or formalist aesthetics.

Celle-ci n'est pas une maison

This, crudely summarized, was the milieu in which the American architect Peter Eisenman was largely formed. A protégé of Rowe's at Cambridge University in the early 1960s, he attracted the attention of the architecture world by the end of that decade with a series of abstract numbered houses. He also functioned as an important impresario, putting together a group of likewise formally inclined architects, the New York Five, and founding a think tank called the Institute for Architecture and Urban Studies in New York, through which the most important European architectural intellectuals, including Leon Krier, would pass during the next decade.

Eisenman's contribution to the discourse of late modernism was to radicalize it, especially through his own mostly unbuilt designs, and beyond anything Rowe himself would ultimately condone—or could have imagined when he initially guided Eisenman to the grail of Giuseppe Terragni's Casa del Fascio in Como. Banishing all lingering guilt for modern architecture's social vocation and immunizing himself against functionalist apologetics, Eisenman embarked on a process of design conceived as a sequence of autonomous and self-generated operations on the language, or more precisely the syntax, of architectural form. With House IV, designed for himself in 1970–71, and extensively elaborated in sketches, drawings, models, and texts both at the time and retrospectively, the series reached a climax with respect to the application of a logical and transformational system of rules. Eisenman's diagrammatic notations detailing the generation of architectural form out of an abstract cubic volume emphasized the oppositional nature of the moves: line versus plane, plane versus volume, symmetry versus asymmetry, end versus side, centrifugal space versus centripetal, exterior versus interior, center versus edge.

A much worked-over text about the house, shredded into horizontal strips and then pieced back together, reproduced in his book *Houses of Cards*, ends with the statement, "This is not a house ~~in the traditional sense~~," its last four words crossed out. Eisenman was seeking to rule out anything extraneous or "extrinsic" in his search for some fundamental Chomskyan "deep structure" or conceptual essence of architecture—a definition that could once and for all distinguish the making of "architecture" from the programmatics of "building" (i.e., the banalities of domestic accommodation and keeping the rain out). This essentialist obsession would subsequently come up against poststructuralism's critique of metaphysics, by which Eisenman would be increasingly affected, especially after falling under the spell of Jacques Derrida. Yet already in the houses that succeeded House IV he began to move from the hyperrationalism of transformational grammar to a method he called "decomposition," acknowledging architecture's indeterminacy as a language and opening himself to a more psychoanalytically inflected approach to the generation of form, or to a dialectic between these two processes.

Degrees of Separation

At the time Eisenman was performing these involuted operations on modernist form, the Luxembourg-born Leon Krier, half a generation his junior, entered the London architectural office of James Stirling, working there from 1968 to 1974. If Eisenman and Krier are invariably portrayed as polemical antagonists who represent polar ideologies with respect to architectural culture—a point to which we shall return—it is important to realize that, at least in terms of their personal itineraries, there exist two very short degrees of separation (or linkage) between them. These are embodied in the figures of Stirling and Rowe, who would both, by the early 1970s, make a full turn from modernism to postmodernism. One might also add, as a matrix for all four, Le Corbusier, the disparities of whose early and late work were differently registered by each.

Indeed, it may be argued that Stirling, with whom Rowe had an especially close relationship, and who articulated his sense of betrayal by the Corbu of Ronchamp and La Tourette in two articles written in the 1950s, undertook a deconstruction of architectural language in the 1960s analogous to Eisenman's. The difference is that while Eisenman concerned himself primarily with architectural syntax, Stirling was preoccupied with semantics. From Leicester Engineering Building (1959–63) through the History Faculty Library at Cambridge (1964–68) and Florey Building at Oxford (1967–71) to Derby Civic Centre (1970), Stirling trafficked in the brutalist and megastructural language of his day while making a travesty of it with technological exaggerations, formal distortions, and increasingly, jarring historical juxtapositions. Krier worked on the Derby scheme, and the incongruous relationship in the drawings between the big barrel-vaulted glass arcade and the classical facade of the existing assembly hall, used as a kind of prop for a portal, announces, as it were, his entry on the scene. Similarly, in Stirling's next project, the Siemens headquarters near Munich (1967–73), the perspective drawings, also bearing the imprint of Krier's witty and cultivated draftsmanship, combine the industrial monumentality of Sant'Elia's Città Nuova with the neoclassicism of Ledoux's Saltworks at Chaux. In their hybrid imagery, Derby and Siemens point the way to the Neue Staatsgalerie at Stuttgart (1977–84), Stirling's postmodernist masterwork.

Absolute Urbanism

Meanwhile, the irascible young Krier, who undoubtedly influenced Stirling during these years at least as much as he was influenced by him, would, upon leaving his office, adopt as absolutist a stance as Eisenman's. If Eisenman defined the purview of architecture in strictly formal terms, Krier defined it strictly in relation to the preindustrial European city. Both thereby became self-appointed custodians of the high culture of architecture—avant-garde and antimodernist respectively—and both rejected as a path for architecture the pop sensibilities of consumer culture, the "vulgar debauch" (in Krier's words) of late-twentieth-century everyday life and the "delirium" (again, Krier's word, apparently used before Rem Koolhaas took possession of it) of its utilitarian urbanism. Inveighing against the aesthetics of fragmentation and historical pastiche that were becoming hallmarks of the new discourse of postmodernism, in the work not just of Stirling but of architects like Robert Venturi, Lucien Kroll, and others, Krier, together with Maurice Culot and his brother Rob Krier, called for a "total" reconstruction of the city along romantic-reactionary lines: the anticapitalism of Ruskin and Morris, European Social Democracy, and (contradictorily, given the previous two) Schinkel-style neoclassicism.

With respect to influence, the same would be true of Rowe as of Stirling: Krier would have a militant effect on Rowe's thinking and would reinforce his increasing hostility to modern architecture. Krier first met Rowe at Cornell in the mid-1970s, after leaving Stirling's office, having been invited to teach there by O. M. Ungers at the same time as Koolhaas. Just as Eisenman's vision of architecture had had a major effect on Rowe fifteen years earlier, Krier now drew the British architectural historian into his own orbit. (Koolhaas, significantly, remained outside this seduction scene, and in fact repaired to the Institute for Architecture and Urban Studies, where he wrote *Delirious New York*, celebrating rather than condemning the savagery of the modern metropolis.) Rowe's feelings for Krier are expressed in a highly affectionate but not unqualified essay of 1984, "The Revolt of the Senses."

In its extremism, Krier's position was, of course, intentionally shocking, and in this regard too it bears affinities to Eisenman's committed and perennial avant-gardism. That the desire to return to the preindustrial world of the eighteenth century was more Luddite than merely nostalgic only gave it greater notoriety, heightened by Krier's talents as both consummate promoter and skilled delineator of his own ideas. (With respect to nostalgia, the opposite is true of Aldo Rossi, whose Chirico-esque recourse to *architettura razionale* was a form of mourning for a past that the Italian architect acknowledged could no longer return.) Moreover, the Krier-Culot politics of "anti-industrial resistance" were (and remain) fundamentally ambiguous as to whether the basic issue is social or aesthetic, that is, whether the criterion for the return to classicism is closer to Loos and Tessenow or to Schinkel and Ledoux.

This same ambiguity regarding means and ends also characterizes Krier's "scandalous" efforts over the years to rehabilitate the Nazi architecture of Albert Speer. To read a piece titled "Vorwärts, Kameraden, Wir Müssen Zurück" (Forward, Comrades, We Must Go Back), originally delivered as an evening lecture at the Institute for Architecture and Urban Studies in 1980 and then published in the journal *Oppositions*, one would think that Hitler's most heinous crime was to accelerate the process of building the autobahn in Germany. (Truth in journalism: my own debut as an architecture critic was provoked by listening to this lecture and writing a somewhat outraged response to it in the same issue of *Oppositions*.) Yet almost as troubling as Krier's effort to uncouple architectural style from architectural culture has been his assumption that the classical idea of architecture is synonymous with some universal and eternal ideal of beauty to which "we" all subscribe—as if to say a painting by Raphael is, objectively speaking, more "beautiful" than one by Mondrian—and related to this, the suggestion that classicism is "by nature" a harmonious, morally regenerative form of architecture that springs from the "citizens" rather than from the power, wealth, and privilege of those who—often brutally—command it to be built.

Such unpleasant realities seem less pressing, to be sure, in Krier's Atlantis project of 1986–88 for the island of Tenerife in the Canaries, in which the humanistic and arcadian ideal of social harmony, ecological balance, and formal perfection receives charming and lyrical expression. Nary an elevator building nor a car nor a computer monitor nor a cell phone mars the long-ago-far-away dreamworld of this resort town on a hill. Commissioned by a German couple as a meeting place for visionary thinkers, artists, and scholars, the project offered Krier an occasion to elaborate his theories about multiuse zoning, pedestrian circulation, antisprawl boundaries, humane scale, Camillo Sitte–inspired vistas and winding streets, and public space. Yet for those who are not willing to jettison their cell phones, Atlantis, like all utopian images, begs to be taken not literally—*pace* Krier—but rather as an evocative reminder and counterimage to the lamentable way things actually are.

Flashforward

It remains necessary to ask why—beyond the historical interest and admitted pleasure of unarchiving two delectable sets of drawings and artifacts—it is worth revisiting these particular projects and polemics of the 1970s and 1980s today. Isn't the confrontation between these two architects famous for their "dangerously" opposing positions *déjà vu*? Isn't, furthermore, the juxtaposition of Eisenman and Krier in the same exhibition gallery a characteristic tactic of an eclectic architectural program, with the effect that one argument neutralizes the other, a little like pouring cold milk into hot coffee?

One suspects that the answer to both questions is partly affirmative. Yet for all this, these two figures remain fascinating and authentic products of the architectural culture of the last forty years. As already suggested and frequently pointed out, they share many similarities: their capacities as polemicists and masters of publicity, their guru relationship to other architects, the uncompromising nature of their positions. They also mirror each other in the inherent contradictions their work embodies. Krier's town of Poundbury, for example, and his role as the pied piper of New Urbanism more generally, attests to the difficulties of reconciling an idealistic desire to construct a communitarian way of life on a global scale with the elitism of the singular and privileged enclave as actually realized. Meanwhile, Eisenman's projects, from his reconstructed armory at the Wexner Center in Ohio to the Holocaust Memorial in Berlin to, most recently, his project for the World Trade Center in New York, reflect the burden on a formalist aesthetic to respond to the representational demands of a semantically loaded (and highly politicized) program; thus the post-Auschwitz poetics of silence have tended at times to be rather noisy.

But the phenomenon of Eisenman and Krier must finally be comprehended as a symptomatic manifestation of a single historical dialectic. Both men emerged out of the disenchantment of late modern architecture, out of the syndrome that Rowe characterizes in his essay on Krier as "the conservatives of Modernism." They represent, in short, diametric responses to the trauma of late capitalist development. It is no small paradox that Krier's urban proposals, despite their anachronistic dress, sustain the original reformist project of modernism more than do Eisenman's aesthetic experiments; while Eisenman's work continues to confront the void of a post–World War II world of form without utopia with the alternative utopia of form itself. So each in his way combats architecture's irrelevance in a world of economic and technological determinism and conducts a critical, passionate, and still poignant battle for its soul.

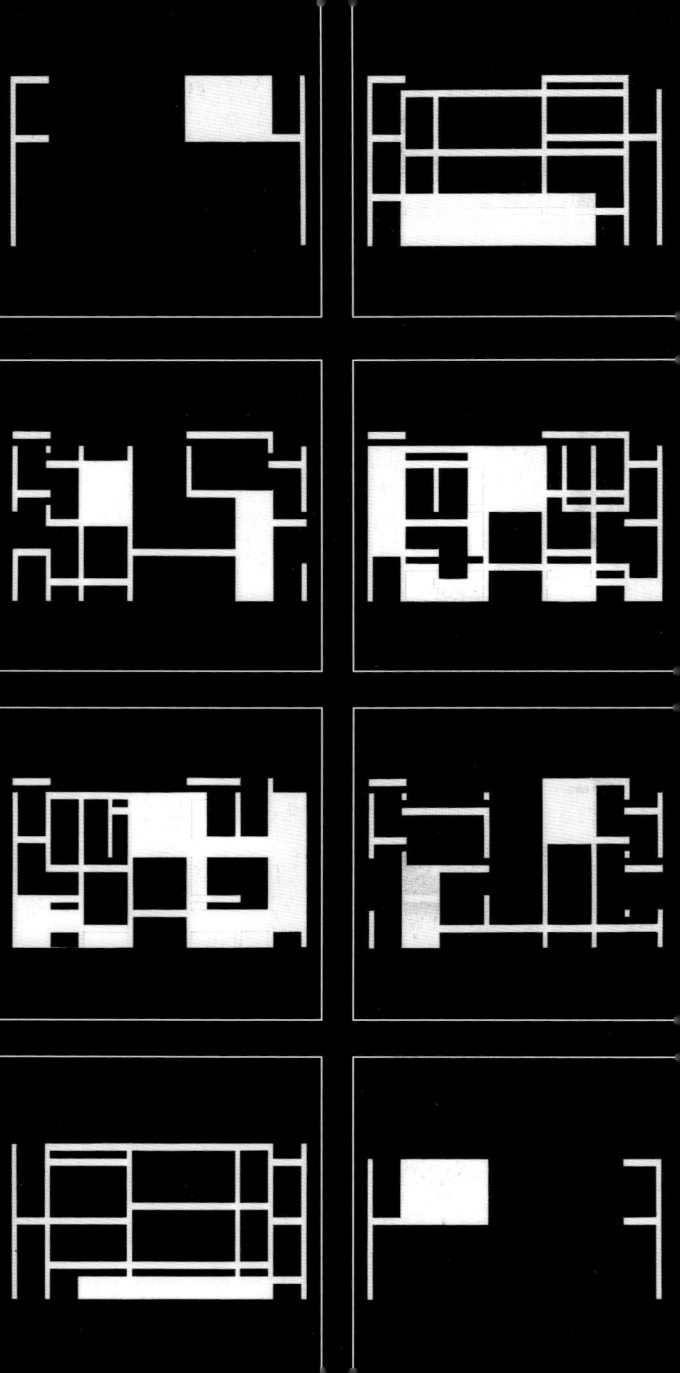

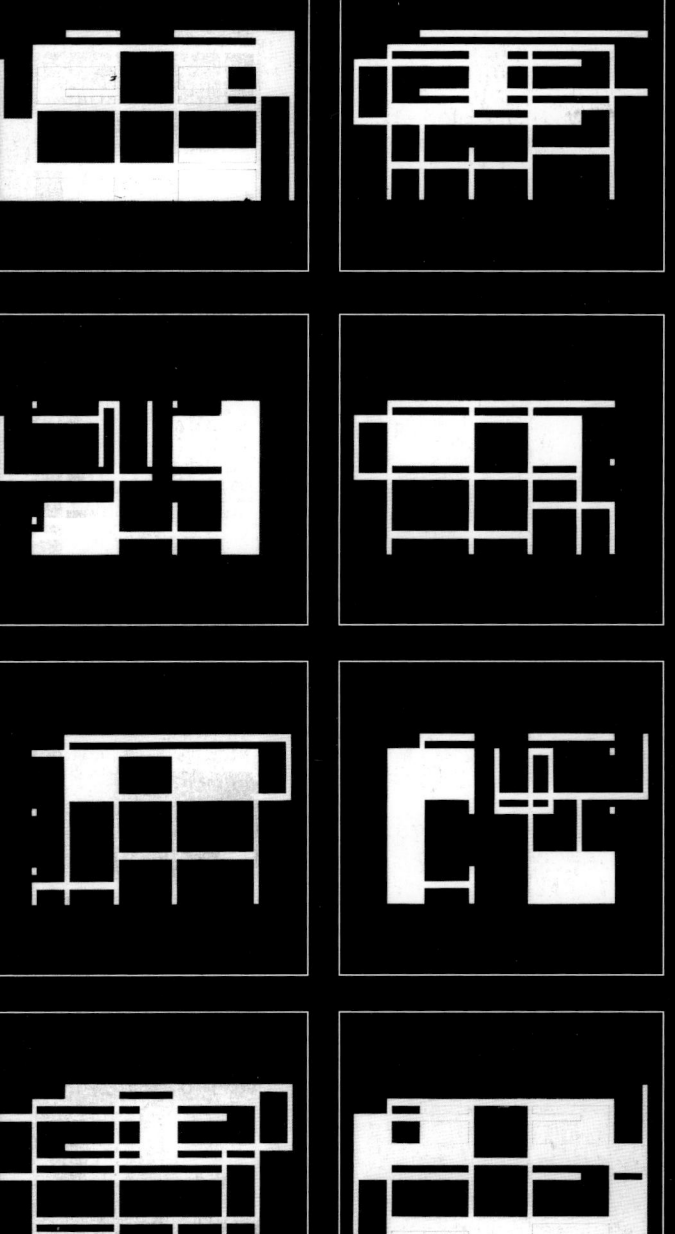

Office of Peter Eisenman, House IV, 1970–71: Sixteen vertical planes, east-west series, south-north series.

"Eisenman/Krier: Two Ideologies," Yale School of Architecture, 2002.

Leon Krier, Atlantis project, 1986–88: model.

Architecture and Ideology

Roger Kimball

The problem of architecture as I see it . . . is the problem of all art—the elimination of the human element from the consideration of form.
—Professor Otto Silenus in Evelyn Waugh's *Decline and Fall*

This meticulous observance of "pure styles" is a mark of failing energy in imagination; it is a mark, also, of an inadequacy in thought: of a failure to define the nature of style in general. We cling in architecture to the pedantries of humanism, because we do not grasp the bearing upon architecture of the humanist ideal.
—Geoffrey Scott, *The Architecture of Humanism*

I was delighted to learn that my presence at Yale's recent symposium about the American architect Peter Eisenman and the Luxembourg-born architect Leon Krier was to be under the aegis of my late friend Brendan Gill. Brendan was a distinguished alumnus of Yale—I trust other alumni will forgive that pleonasm—and he was also widely admired as a keen, lively writer about architecture for the *New Yorker*.

Brendan was a merry soul. It is pleasing to speculate about what his reaction would have been to the news that Robert A. M. Stern, the dean of the School of Architecture, had decided not only to ask me to introduce this symposium but also to denominate me, if but momentarily, the Brendan Gill Lecturer. I suspect that his response would have been one of amusement—spiced, perhaps, with a soupçon of anxiety.

Since I happened to be in New Haven while the exhibition of Mr. Eisenman's and Mr. Krier's work from the 1970s and 1980s was being installed, I took advantage of the coincidence to get a glimpse of the exhibition as it went up. It is one of the privileges of being a critic that one often has the opportunity to drop in as an exhibition is being mounted. There is always a certain excitement, a certain freshness, about seeing an exhibition in this state of morning dishabille, as it were. The bustle of technicians fixing labels, touching up the paint, making some late decisions about exactly how that last row of pictures should be hung is somehow more energizing than distracting. It's like a glimpse backstage at a theatrical performance, which to my mind tends rather to enhance than to dissipate the magic of the performance.

I thought about Brendan as I picked my way gingerly among the ladders, drills, track lighting, and masking tape. I wish that he could have accompanied me. He would, I think, have had a smile for the images on the wall and a twinkle in his eye for the symposium as a whole. Brendan liked handsome pictures, and he had a healthy appetite for incongruity. He would not have been disappointed on either score.

The welcoming image in the exhibition is a copy of one of Mr. Krier's classical fantasies. It is a sort of acropolis populated by friends and patrons besporting themselves in contemporary garb: Puvis de Chavannes with couture by Ralph Lauren, sets by Winckelmann. It would, I think, have brought Brendan up short. "Do you suppose it is meant seriously?" he might have whispered, amusement once again competing with anxiety.

Now, Brendan liked his bit of kitsch as much as the next chap, but he preferred it light and gently self-mocking. There is a mocking quality to some of the images on view in this exhibition; there is certainly a mocking quality in some of the architectural visions that the exhibition represents; but it is a mockery directed outward, toward the viewer, toward the public, not inward, toward the maker. The great social theorist Phineas Taylor Barnum is alleged to have remarked, "There's a sucker born every minute." Although a proof of this proposition awaits definitive formulation, "Eisenman/Krier: Two Ideologies" deserves an honored place in the annals of corroborative incident.

Still, there are a lot of fetching images on view in this exhibition. Mr. Krier is more than an accomplished architectural draftsman: he is a brilliantly evocative artist whose classicizing fantasies are a delight to the eye and a spur to the imagination. His drawings are something more—something other, at any rate—than attractive building instructions or architectural elevations. They are tranquil portraits of—I was going to say of a vanished world, but perhaps it would be more accurate to say that they are reconstructions of a world that never quite existed, indeed that never could exist, but whose beauty, whose seductiveness, lies precisely in that mixture of impossibility and exquisite delineation.

Mr. Eisenman, of course, does not go in much for seducing his viewers—not, anyway, with promises of any normal gratification. But considered simply as drawings—that is, considered apart from any alleged connection with the art of architecture—the plans and sketches for the unbuilt House IV possess their own beauty and fascination. It is naturally a very different sort of fascination from that exerted by Mr. Krier's drawings. They are cooler, less sumptuous, less immediately welcoming than Mr. Krier's classical essays. They bear the stamp not of an artist's hand but of a puzzle-maker's ingenuity, and they do this by design. Mr. Krier elaborates a way of life; Mr. Eisenman analyzes—or seems to analyze—a geometry. His drawings are fiercely, indeed ostentatiously, cerebral. It is, from one point of view, good fun, and it should be acknowledged, Mr. Eisenman expresses his vision with considerable elegance. A cube is presented; it is bisected; it is hollowed out; the cube is rotated, inverted, elaborated, and transformed by a series of algorithms. This prodigy Mr. Eisenman tells us it is a house. Some people believe him. He says House IV is "an attempt to alienate the individual from the known way in which he perceives and understands his environment." Rich Canadians stand in awe and shovel money his way. Universities appoint him to the faculty. Learned seminars are devoted to dissecting his importance. How it would have gratified Mr. Barnum.

Alice Roosevelt Longworth famously said, "If you can't say something good about someone, sit right here by me." I confess that I have always harbored a sneaking fondness for Alice. But by and large Brendan belonged to the opposite school. He tended to look on the bright side. He much preferred liking things to disliking them. I have no doubt that he would have found a good deal to like in "Eisenman/Krier: Two Ideologies." In purely visual terms there is a good deal to like. But I suspect that, like me, he would have greeted the proposition that this was an exhibition whose chief concern was with architecture with a certain skepticism.

Why the skepticism? I believe that the subtitle of this symposium—"Two Ideologies"—may have a useful clue to at least part of the answer. It is, I think, a spectacularly apt subtitle. For with these two architects we really are dealing not simply with radically different approaches to architecture but with two opposing ideologies.

The literature accompanying this symposium suggests that the planners were interested chiefly in exploring that opposition—exploring, that is to say, the discontinuities that define Mr. Eisenman's and Mr. Krier's relationship to the tradition of modernism and to each other. I will have something to say about that in due course. First I invite you to ponder what it might mean to say that an architect espouses an *ideology*.

Of course architects, like lesser mortals, might espouse or exhibit an ideology in their capacity as individual political agents. But what does it mean to say that an architect, considered in his capacity as an architect, espouses an ideology? Think about it: Did Brunelleschi have an ideology? Did Alberti? Did Stanford White? They certainly had opinions about what made good architecture: they embraced some things and disparaged others. But having an opinion is not the same thing as espousing an architectural ideology.

Modernism was notoriously an architecture that never left home without a manifesto, and doubtless some practitioners of modernist architecture would count as ideological architects. Or one might point to Albert Speer, whose grandiose neoclassicism was self-consciously put in the service of an ideology. It is perhaps significant in this context that Mr. Krier has had some admiring things to say about Speer's architecture—not, I hasten to add, because of its association with the Nazis but because of its effort to revivify, in hypertrophied form, a certain version of neoclassicism.

But what, to step back for a moment, *is* an ideology? We live at a time when we are regularly assured that "everything is political," that everyone and everything has an ideology, that no point of view is "innocent," that "truth" is merely an honorific conferred by power, and so forth. But let's leave that self-contradictory, mind-numbing lit-crit-shtick to one side. It doesn't bring us any closer to understanding the title "Eisenman/Krier: Two Ideologies."

The word *idéologie* seems to have been coined by the French nobleman Destutt de Tracy in 1796. Destutt, a follower of the materialist philosopher Condillac, had set out to describe the process by which ideas came to consciousness. He was a sort of proto-sociologist. But although the word, like so many dubious intellectual imports, is of French origin, it did not acquire its full quota of owlishness until it was adopted and groomed by the Germans. Marx and Engels did more than anyone to popularize the term. It was while at school with the Marxists that the word *ideology* turned nasty and developed teeth. Characteristically, the word acquired a dual meaning: overtly, it was just a fancy term for describing someone's world view, but by insinuation, it also cast a negative penumbra, a suggestion of rigidity or "false-consciousness," as the Marxists say. More and more, "an ideology" was understood to describe an unfortunate piece of mental—and even moral—baggage that one's opponents labored under but that did not much bother right-thinking—by which I mean left-leaning—souls.

The word *ideology* has never quite lost its Marxist accent; it continues to carry with it the hint of subterranean forces at work—forces that only the initiated are in a position to discern and emancipate themselves from. Indeed, that aura of impermeable knowingness is an important reason that *ideology* is such a popular word in the academy. Still, continual use has smoothed some of its rough edges. One can thus have a title like "Eisenman/Krier: Two Ideologies" without people thinking you are being rude.

In *The Origins of Totalitarianism*, Hannah Arendt observes that an ideology differs from a simple opinion in that an ideology claims to possess "the key to history" or "intimate knowledge" of "hidden universal laws." Dilute this a bit further and you wind up with ideology in the sense we have it here: "Eisenman/Krier: Two Ideologies"—that is, two efforts to recast architecture on the basis of a specialized program or agenda that takes its cue as much from extra-architectural considerations as from architectural ones.

What is the nature of those programs or agendas? In the case of Mr. Eisenman, I believe, it revolves largely around an ambition to uncover a hitherto concealed "essence" of architecture. In the case of Mr. Krier—at least in his work during the years that this symposium focuses on—the ideology revolves around an attempt to redefine architecture as a sort of classicizing mythopoesis or mythmaking.

Let's start with Mr. Eisenman. House IV is one of six similarly abstract houses that he designed in the 1960s and 1970s. The fact that they are known only by Roman numerals adds to their forbidding aura. A book called *Houses of Cards*, published in the late 1980s, is devoted to these works. In an essay he published in this volume, Mr. Eisenman writes that "the essence of the act of architecture is the dislocation of an ever-reconstituting metaphysic of architecture." In case that was unclear, Mr. Eisenman goes on to explain that the designs for the six houses were all "governed by the intent to define the act of architecture as the dislocation of consequent reconstitution of an ever-accruing metaphysic of architecture."

At this stage of his career, anyway, Mr. Eisenman was very fond of the word *metaphysic*. In the course of his essay, readers are introduced not only to the "metaphysic of architecture" but also to the "metaphysic of the center," the "metaphysic of the house," even the "metaphysic of dining."

It would, I think, be a mistake to regard such formidable phrases as extraneous verbal curlicues. The point is that experience of Peter Eisenman's architecture is partly a *rhetorical* experience. Architecture is not itself a verbal medium, as Mr. Eisenman sometimes pretends, but his own architectural efforts are incomplete without the accompanying text. When we encounter a stairway that leads nowhere, as we do at the Wexner Center for the Arts in Columbus, Ohio, we need his help to understand that we are being given a lesson in linguistic futility. Otherwise we might foolishly conclude that it was just a stairway that led nowhere and wonder about the sanity of the chap who paid the architect's bill.

Mr. Eisenman was once a recherché taste. But he has, in recent years, become something of a celebrity, and so his little lessons have become quite familiar. For the benefit of those who have not experienced his act, however, I feel I should provide at least one full-fledged example. Regarding the "metaphysic of dining," Mr. Eisenman tells us that House III and House IV explore

> *an alternative process of making occupiable form, . . . a process specifically developed to operate as freely as possible from functional considerations. From a traditional point of view, several columns "intrude on" and "disrupt" the living and dining areas as a result of this process . . . Nonetheless, these dislocations . . . have, according to the occupants of the house, changed the dining experience in a real and, more importantly, unpredictable fashion.*

Being of a charitable disposition, I do not propose to analyze this passage. Instead, I present it as an artwork in its own right, something that is better admired for its autonomous beauty than picked over for its meaning. Such passages are best regarded as rhetorical adjuncts of Mr. Eisenman's drawings and buildings: frames without whose support his work could not even appear to us *as* architecture. Still, it does seem worth noting that although the occupants of Mr. Eisenman's houses may have found that his provocatively placed columns have *changed*—even changed "unpredictably"—their experience of living and dining, Mr. Eisenman does not say that their experience was made any more *pleasant*. Far from it. One of the main goals of Mr. Eisenman's architecture is to subvert anything so bourgeois as comfort or intelligibility. As he puts it, his houses

> *attempt to have little to do with the traditional and existing metaphysic of the house, the physical and psychological gratification associated with the traditional form of the house, . . . in order to initiate a search for those possibilities of dwelling that may have been repressed by that metaphysic.*

With respect to leaving behind "physical and psychological gratification," I think we can judge Mr. Eisenman's houses an unqualified success. As for "dwelling"—well, the word has a gratifying Heideggerian ring to it. But what about the "repressed possibilities" of dwelling? Could it be that there are some things that *should* be repressed? Might it be the case that, if there are such things as repressed possibilities of dwelling, it is to our benefit that they *stay* repressed? I suppose it could be said that Mr. Eisenman exposed one repressed possibility of dwelling when he left a few holes in the second-story floor of one of his houses. In that case, one repressed possibility was a broken leg or a broken neck, and the occupants of the house, as we read in a recent article about Mr. Eisenman in the *New York Times*, quickly saw to it that this "possibility of dwelling" was firmly re-repressed through the expediency of some metal grates fitted over the holes.

Let us turn now to Mr. Krier. At first blush, he seems to present a kinder, gentler face to the world than Mr. Eisenman. At least, it is a less cerebral face. Mr. Krier's stairways lead somewhere, his floors are solid, his facades have the pleasing aspect of old friends. He offers a *Masterpiece Theatre* sort of coziness—stately homes, lots of pillars and classical cornices—and one assumes that the servant problem is well under control. If Peter Eisenman is engaged in a search for the essence of architecture, Mr. Krier is engaged in a search for its Arcady, a dreamy version of its idealized form.

Although the portion of the Yale exhibition devoted to Mr. Krier's work is centered on the Atlantis project, an unbuilt, classically decorated retreat for artists and intellectuals, it includes a wide range of drawings by Mr. Krier. Most pertain to unbuilt projects. Of course, many visionary architects have specialized in unbuilt projects: one thinks of Ledoux, Boullée, Piranesi, and others. Furnishing the imagination with possibilities—even, if I may so put it, *impossible* possibilities—has been a fertile source of architectural activity since the Tower of Babel—or perhaps even the bowers populating the Garden of Eden. Still, Mr. Krier embraces the unbuilt with a special passion.

A common thread running through many of his projects is rejection: rejection not only of modernist architecture but of modern reality. It's a small-is-beautiful, natural-materials, brown-rice, and no-curtain-wall sort of philosophy—attractive to elites who can afford to dream those dreams—and why not? Some twenty years ago, Mr. Krier famously summed up this ethic of rejection when he declared: "A responsible architect cannot possibly build today . . . Building can only mean a greater or smaller degree of collaboration in a civilized society's process of self-destruction." Mr. Krier has apparently repudiated that statement. Nevertheless, it underscores a permanent temptation to which his approach to architecture is susceptible. Nor was that statement a solitary aberration. "I can only make Architecture," he said in another manifesto-like statement from the 1970s, "because I do not build. I do not build because I am an Architect."

With those declarations in mind, it is interesting to consider the developments that Mr. Krier collaborated on in Seaside, Florida, and Poundbury, England: do such New Urbanist experiments count as upper-case-A Architecture, lower-case-a architecture, or something else entirely? And what about Mr. Krier? Was he an Architect or an architect while working on those projects? Maybe he wasn't an architect at all, but something else entirely? And here's a further worry: if only those who do not build can make Architecture, what about those who *have built*? Can they go back to being Architects after a certain period of abstinence? Or is being an Architect like virginity: a quality that, once lost, is gone forever?

I do not pretend to know the answers to these questions. But I raise them because I think they point to an element in Leon Krier's work that has not perhaps been sufficiently noticed. Mr. Krier has often been described as a historicist; he is that. But he is a historicist with a powerful commitment to purity, to an idealism that is moral as much as architectural. Throughout his work there is a conscious effort to evoke a more humanized future by reimagining the past. Mr. Krier dislikes the word *utopian*. But there is a reason that one finds it cropping up so often in discussions of his work. In the face of an unsatisfactory reality—a reality populated by ugly buildings, too many people, and pollution; in other words, *our* reality—he composes highly personal versions of tradition that seek more to liberate the imagination than to describe a definite task. One attractive side of this vision is to be found in all those pretty pictures of classically faced buildings. I have not myself been to Seaside or Poundbury, but I am willing to believe that those boutique showpieces are plenty *mignon*, too.

But in fact those developments represent Mr. Krier in a conciliatory, compromising mood. And according to some reports, he was not at all happy with the results at Poundbury: too many concessions to vulgarity. In any event, more typical—more typical of the work highlighted by this symposium, anyway—are fantasies like the Atlantis project or his plan to scratch Washington, D.C., and turn it into four Georgetown-sized villages in which pedestrian traffic would be moderated by such expedients as flooding the Washington Mall.

If there seems to be a touch of megalomania about such projects, well, Mr. Krier once spoke of facing up to "the colossal and almost inhuman task of *global ecological reconstruction*." Around the same time, he also remarked that the criterion for his work is contained in a question: "If I had to design the whole world, what would I do?" This was a contingency that Mr. Krier, only half-jokingly, described as "not improbable."

I have rehearsed what I take to be certain central aspects of Mr. Eisenman's ideology and Mr. Krier's ideology in order to delineate the basic shape or thrust of their architectural vision. I have left a lot out of this account. For example, there are other aspects to Mr. Eisenman's activity besides the search for the essence of architecture. A skeptical observer, noting such things as the holes in the floors of his house, the small windows at ankle level in offices he has designed, the stairways that go nowhere, the plans he offers for Ground Zero that include office buildings that look like half-squashed paper bags, might wonder whether Mr. Eisenman was really in earnest.

Years ago, Philip Johnson extolled postmodernism for having insinuated "the giggle" into architecture. Is it possible that Mr. Eisenman—who after all is a late beneficiary of Philip Johnson's activities as an architectural impresario—is it possible that he, too, is a giggle-making postmodernist? Only, having found all the slots for cheerful historical pastiche occupied, he took the next best opening and specialized in angry-looking send-ups of Corbusier and Terragni? Is Mr. Eisenman, too, in the business of purveying architectural spoofs? Perhaps, like other sensible people, he knows deep down that Jacques Derrida is a French fog-making machine whose opinions about language and architecture are no less risible than they are mystifying. I mention it as a possibility worth considering.

Mr. Krier is a bit harder to get in focus. Having started his professional life as a disciple of James Stirling, he seems to have vacillated between the role of architectural gadfly or prophet—"Repent! The end of the curtain wall is nigh!"—and the role of pragmatic urban planner who is trying to get the Prince of Wales's business done.

It was one of the assumptions of the Yale symposium that, in the 1970s and 1980s, Mr. Eisenman and Mr. Krier were both, in their disparate ways, reacting against modernism. Maybe they were. But I am not sure how illuminating that observation is. At least since Robert Venturi inverted Mies van der Rohe and proclaimed the gospel of "Less is a bore," elite architects have been hopping onto the antimodernist bandwagon faster than you can say Colin Rowe. And some of them have done hugely attractive work. But Mr. Eisenman and Mr. Krier stand out or stand apart from most antimodernist architects, and so I am not sure how instructive it would be to explore their "dissimilar perceptions of history," as the program for the Yale symposium invited us to do.

How else can we understand their activity? One possibly fruitful parallel that occurred to me comes from the world of ethology, of animal behavior. Readers of Konrad Lorenz's fascinating books on the subject will remember his discussion of what he calls a "vacuum activity." A vacuum activity is instinctual behavior that occurs when an animal, deprived of its normal surroundings and objects, nevertheless "goes through the motions" of some activity typical of its species. Lorenz provides several examples from the bird kingdom. Many city dwellers who own dogs will have witnessed another example. Long deprived of bones and dirt, a city-living dog will pretend to bury a nonexistent bone in nonexistent dirt in the corner of a room. Burying bones is instinctive behavior for dogs, and a boneless, dirtless life is just not to be borne. After a certain period of time sans bones and sans dirt, this behavior "discharges" itself, in Lorenz's term, and we find Fido pawing earnestly at the carpet in the corner of the living room.

I wonder whether the intriguing concept of a vacuum activity sheds some light on the relevant work of Mr. Eisenman and Mr. Krier. After all, much of what we are presented with in this exhibition is unbuilt—surely a frustrating contingency for men whose profession is building things. Just as a dog "buries" a nonexistent "bone," so Mr. Eisenman "designs" a "house" and Mr. Krier "plans" a fantasy "island."

I am sorry that we cannot engage Konrad Lorenz as a consultant in this case. I suspect he might discover some useful extensions to his idea of a vacuum activity. Is there, for example, such a thing as a *half-vacuum activity*—just a bit of air hissing in—in which, for example, a dog has a bone but no dirt, or an architect builds a house that turns out to be uninhabitable? I do not know. It is a question that demands more research, and probably a government grant. I cannot help thinking that the idea of the vacuum activity may be illuminating for architectural ideologies in which futility is budgeted in as either a basic design element or a necessary adjunct of its impracticality.

The issue of futility brings me—a bit late admittedly—to my own title. I've settled here on "Architecture and Ideology." Originally, though, I had something more baroque. When I accepted Dean Stern's invitation to participate in the symposium, he instantly asked for a title for my remarks. After a bit of cogitation, I wrote back and offered "Is There Architecture after Modernism?" I thought that might be appropriate for a discussion of work that is not only self-consciously antimodernist but that also raises the question of the future of architecture, in one instance by subverting traditional architectural practice, in the other by fetishizing it. As an afterthought, I told Dean Stern that I'd considered proposing, in deference to Mr. Eisenman, something like—please note the parentheses— "(Re)Positioning Architecture: (Post)Modernism, (Re)Presentation, and the Discourses of (Dis)Play." Dean Stern replied that he favored the longer title—it was, he suggested, "more provocative." I saw his point. "Is There Architecture after Modernism?" is *moderately* provocative because it raises the possibility that there isn't any architecture after modernism, which is clearly absurd. But the longer title has the advantage of total unintelligibility, which I know is in some circles a powerful recommendation.

Still, that original title was not merely flippant. The first bit poses what I think is a serious question. My answer to the question is, No, there isn't architecture after modernism—if by "modernism" we understand not a certain denuded style of building but rather the social, economic, and political givens of contemporary life. Various English statesmen, from Gladstone to Sir William Harcourt, have been credited with the observation that "We are all socialists now." Alas, you might say—well, *I* would say "alas." But there it is. That is simply a statement of how things are. You might lament it but you cannot change it.

Similarly, there is an important sense in which we are all modernists now, Mr. Krier as much as Gordon Bunshaft. It doesn't matter whether you favor curtain walls or Corinthian columns, jeweled concrete or cedar shakes. The issue is not modernism or antimodernism but good architecture versus bad architecture. If the architecture we have been accustomed to calling modernist errs in the direction of severity and hyperrationalism, much of the architecture that has arisen to challenge it has erred in the direction of silliness, grim or fatuous as the case may be.

Which is worse? Stock in the modernist enterprise has been unnaturally depressed for some time now, and so it is worth reminding ourselves that there are plenty of great modernist success stories—the Yale Art Gallery by Louis Kahn, for example, or the Yale Center for British Art, its younger cousin across the street.

I believe that if we are to get a fruitful perspective on the opposition in the title "Eisenman/Krier: Two Ideologies," we need to put that opposition in a wider context. One way of doing that allows me to introduce the hero of this lecture, the English architect and architectural historian Geoffrey Scott. Most people interested in architecture will know of Scott. He is the author of a deservedly famous book. *The Architecture of Humanism* was first published in 1914 and instantly attained the status of a classic. I bring up *The Architecture of Humanism* because, although it is in one sense well known, its fundamental messages seem to have been forgotten. It is the old story of familiarity breeding, if not contempt, exactly, then at least neglect.

It might seem odd to introduce Geoffrey Scott into a discussion of work by Peter Eisenman and Leon Krier. After all, the ostensible subject of *The Architecture of Humanism* is Renaissance architecture. But Scott's subtitle—"A Study in the History of Taste"—points to the book's larger purview. Its pertinence extends to the practice and appreciation of architecture generally.

Scott has two sets of lessons for us. The first revolves around his distillation of Vitruvius's principles of architecture. Vitruvius had a clutch of seven or eight; Scott, quoting the Renaissance poet Henry Wotton, boils them down to three: commodity, firmness, and delight, or as we might put it, comfort and serviceability, craftsmanship and solidity, and beauty. These are the principles that must be observed in order to achieve what Wotton called "well-building."

Scott's second set of lessons revolves around the series of "fallacies" he enumerates. Especially important in this context are the romantic fallacy, whose most typical form, Scott tells us, is "the cult of the extinct," and the fallacies detailed in the chapter "The Academic Tradition." Scott was himself an apostle of traditional architectural order. But he noted that although order is good, it is not by itself sufficient for good architecture. "Many of the ugliest patterns and most joyless buildings," he wrote, "possess order in a high degree; they exhibit fixed and evident ratios of design." But because they lack the animating leaven of taste, they fail.

What is the gravamen of taste? In a word, it is the body. Again and again, Scott came back to the importance of the human body as the indispensable measure in architecture. The needs and dispositions of the human spirit incarnate—which means both a body in space and a body registering, contemplating space—provide the measure of that bedrock architectural value, the appropriate.

Scott speaks partly as a historian of architecture and partly as a custodian of the humanist values that were articulated with luxurious richness in Renaissance architecture. This is why the lasting value of his book is not as an antiquarian relic but as an ever contemporary inspiration. The humanist values for which Scott enlists architecture are as pertinent today as they were in 1914—or for that matter, 1419. All of us have heard trendy architects and their apologists natter on about Michel Foucault, the advent of the "post-human," and the impossibility of coherence or stability. But that is the twittering of sterility and exhaustion. As Scott noted, "Space affects us and can control our spirit . . . The architect models in space as a sculptor in clay. He designs his space as a work of art; that is, he attempts through its means to excite a certain mood in those who enter it."

That is as true for us as it was for Brunelleschi or Alberti. And like them, we too possess what Scott calls "the humanist instinct," which "looks in the world for physical conditions that are related to our own, for movements which are like those we enjoy, for resistances that resemble those that can support us, for a setting where we should be neither lost nor thwarted."

Catering to that "humanist instinct" in the medium of space is the vocation of architecture. There is an aesthetic component to this project: a component satisfied in the pleasing arrangement of masses, lines, shadows, and spaces. But the essential neediness and incompleteness of the human condition guarantees that architecture can never be judged by aesthetic criteria alone. "Architecture," as Scott put it, "is subservient to the general uses of mankind." We approach architecture with what Scott, echoing the famous Kantian formula, calls a "disinterested desire for beauty," but this desire is tethered by continual reference to the quotidian inventory of physical, psychological, and social imperatives.

If we compare Scott's humanism with the ideologies of Mr. Eisenman and Mr. Krier, we may distill several principles or, if that seems too grand a term, admonitions. One is what I like to refer to as the Amis principle, after the British novelist Kingsley Amis. It reads "Nice things are nicer than nasty ones." A simple principle, that—but consider how often it has been forgotten or indeed deliberately sabotaged by people who believe that notoriety can successfully substitute for genuine artistic accomplishment.

This leads naturally to my second admonition, which I take from Alberti. "Never let greed for glory," Alberti says at the end of Book Nine of *On Architecture*, "impel you to embark rashly on anything that is unusual or without precedent." That is a sentiment that might profitably be chiseled into the lintel over the entrance of Paul Rudolph's Art and Architecture Building at Yale.

The third admonition concerns what we might call the "pudding test": architecture must be not only looked at but lived with, indeed lived in, and so what works marvelously on paper may fail utterly on the street. The proof of architecture is concrete, not abstract. Seductive theories do not necessarily produce gratifying buildings.

The fourth admonition addresses what we might call novelty architecture. When someone erects a hot dog stand in the shape of a giant hot dog, the result may be in bad taste—maybe comic bad taste—but no great harm is done. The problem is that more and more architecture is coming to resemble novelty architecture. I don't mean that architects are slavishly mimetic. But novelty architecture comes in several varieties. Is a building that allegedly illustrates linguistic vertigo any less preposterous than the hot dog stand? How about something that could have come from the set for *Ben Hur*? Novelty architecture has a place; even Geoffrey Scott would admit that, I think. Only we need to keep it in its place: roadside refectories, amusement parks, universities, and other retreats from the serious business of life.

The last admonition I will mention is perhaps the most important. It concerns the question of essence, the ambition to exhibit or explore "the essence of architecture"—as if a house stripped bare somehow revealed the inner reality of a house. It is one of the virtues of the humanist instinct to recognize that the human world is—*essentially* is—something more than a distillation of essences. It is, on the contrary, a world of appearances: of how things look and comport themselves. This is something that our culture, and our architecture, has largely lost sight of, to our very great diminishment. The philosopher Roger Scruton has dilated on this point in his writings about architecture. "There is," Mr. Scruton writes, "no greater error in the study of human things than to believe that the search for what is essential must lead us to what is hidden." Mr. Scruton is hardly an aesthete: indeed, he follows Ruskin in insisting that art and culture are "not detachable, in the last analysis, from piety." But part of that piety is acknowledging our deep submission to the superficial, to the realm of appearance. This is the profound wisdom contained in Oscar Wilde's apparently flippant remark that only a very shallow person does not judge by appearances.

There is a largely retrospective, even autumnal, ingredient in the current celebration of work by Peter Eisenman and Leon Krier. We are invited to look back a couple of decades or more to explore the work of two energetic architects whose words and whose work helped set the agenda for important aspects of contemporary architectural theory and practice. It is, in all senses of the word, heady stuff, full of breathtaking ideas. Are they, for all that, *good* ideas? Well, I will leave you all to answer that question—or to leave it unanswered if that course seems more expedient. Leaving it unanswered, I suspect, is what Brendan Gill would have done, if for no other reason than he wanted to keep the fun of architecture going as long as possible. Fun is nice. I like fun. But fun remains most fun when it keeps to its appropriate place. The ambition to transform all of life into a playground is a prescription for the ruin of fun. Brendan knew this, too, fortunately. I am convinced that he would have approved of my concluding quotation, from the nineteenth-century American historian William Hickling Prescott: "The surest test of the civilization of a people is to be found in their architecture, which presents so noble a field for the display of the grand and the beautiful; and which, at the same time, is so intimately connected with the essential comforts of life." It's a lot to live up to. But the alternative is having a lot to live down.

Eisenman and Krier:

A Conversation

This conversation was originally published in the February 1983 issue of *Skyline*, issued by Rizzoli International Publications for the Institute for Architecture and Urban Studies. The interview was edited by Margot Jacqz.

PETER EISENMAN I believe you are one of the few architects who possess what could be called an architectural theology. Could you explain the tenets of this theology? How would you describe it in terms of the moral position that you seem to hold in relation to society and to the role of the architect?

LEON KRIER Because of the astounding material progress of the last centuries, many people are convinced that mankind, while growing older and stronger, has also become more intelligent. One forgets too easily that while units of muscle power can be combined to make ever more powerful machines, units of gray matter cannot be accumulated to create anything more intelligent than an individual brain. Intelligence and moral courage are neither desirable nor expandable beyond certain limits.

Philosophy and theology are the sciences of those limits, and therefore, they are extremely useful crutches in times of confusion: they help us with what we strive to understand but cannot possibly ever understand.

As far as the universal aspects of architecture and other subjects are concerned, they tell us what architecture must be but cannot possibly be. By extension, then, we understand architecture's means and ends and what our duties and pleasures may be. Philosophy and theology—as is true of any theoretical reflections—are not goals but mere instruments that allow us to clearly distinguish *universal ideas* in a confusion of *particular phenomena;* to separate what is eternal and what is temporal; more superficially, to know what is a principle and what is a deception. In times of decadence, only rare individuals take on the task of thinking. That is what I believe I have to do.

EISENMAN You said that one goal of theology is to define the realm of human ability in terms of doing and thinking. But man has traditionally defined himself in terms of God and nature—that is, within a triadic cosmology. In these terms, theocentrism proposed a hierarchy with God as the mediator between man and nature; anthropocentrism proposed man as the mediator between God and nature; finally, biocentrism proposed nature as mediator. Today, with the potential for complete nuclear destruction of civilization, there is an objective technocentrism in which external forces outside of man's control have assumed a position in the system. It is no longer possible to return to an anthropocentric cosmology. That is a nostalgia for a hopeful future. Our theology must respond to new limits.

This is a simple reality that we have to talk about—not in architectural terms but, first, in theological terms. With these new limitations, we now have what I would call a "futureless present." I would accuse you of refusing to accept—or of not addressing—the present definition of man's situation in this new cosmology.

KRIER We cannot talk of a new cosmology when we can find only fragmented conceptions of life.

EISENMAN That, however, implies anarchy, which is not order.

KRIER Yes, it is. The more individual conceptions differ, the more they are the same; they have their fragmentary nature in common.

EISENMAN But the intermingling of fragments is a different philosophy than the traditional hierarchical philosophy, which evolved from a hierarchical understanding of the universe.

KRIER If I break a cup, I am left with fragments. I can re-create the cup by gluing the pieces together again. You would probably say that that is going back. That is absolutely correct, and that is what I am doing with architecture.

EISENMAN Our only recourse is to glue the cup back together?

KRIER Yes. I believe Plato's conception of ideas is very useful: the human brain can only conceive of and work with a limited number of ideas. Architecture and the city are one set of ideas, but with this limited set one can fabricate an infinite number of real buildings. There can be no building, no culture worth speaking of, without constant reference to these fundamental and simple ideas.

Skeptics believe that there are no universal ideas, only a multitude of facts and phenomena; that there is no morality, only individual mores. That is an attitude that allows you to look at the past and consume whatever you can see and grasp. It certainly does not help you to create objects or even to have decent manners.

EISENMAN I do not want to disagree with that. My point was that nature, the third pole of the cosmological triad, has changed. Man has unleashed nature— maybe accidentally—and can no longer necessarily control it. Modernism reflected individual anxiety and the person alienated from society. But today we have a society of people born after 1945 who subconsciously feel that there has been a fundamental change—a collective anxiety. What can be done when people are in fear of not living out their natural lives? How do you accommodate that collective terror?

One could say my "theology" is based on the fact that I do not believe in the historicist view of history as continuous, with the past willing the present and predicting the future. I believe history is marked by stops and starts, ruptures. During the Renaissance, or the Enlightenment, for example, or during the period of modern architecture, something happened, something changed. We are now, without question, in a period after modernism—a period with changed sensibilities.

The cup cannot be glued back together if there is no glue. The changed condition of nature has taken the glue away. I do not deny that the cup is there, the fragments are there, and even your will to glue it back together is there. I would argue, however, that you no longer have the option of gluing the cup back together because either there is no water to put in it or there is no glue. That is what I call a change in the cosmology. Leon, no glue, no water: fragments.

KRIER The trouble with the broken cup is not the lack of glue but the lack of will to glue it.

EISENMAN The will exists.

KRIER No, it does not. Otherwise we would mend the pieces.

EISENMAN How? You cannot glue a cup together with will.

KRIER Ideas do not actually break. They may be forgotten and rediscovered. They are by nature perfect and indestructible. In the world of things, however, there can be no perfection and everything is destructible.

EISENMAN That is a classical notion. In a classical mode of thought there are only unitary ideas. But now, because the elements of cosmology are no longer the same, we cannot return to the spirit that motivated the *will* to wholeness; we must still acknowledge the existence of the fracture.

KRIER You are addressing here the existential questions posed by the last few generations. I was born after 1945 and I have no problems with "going back." I am not proposing to revive old problems and injustices, but to use the most intelligent and best solutions of the past. Ideas have no past and no future; they are ever present. "Going back" is only a manner of speaking. I am talking about the memory of worthwhile experiences and ideas.

EISENMAN But why do you not admit in your theology that there has been a change in cosmology? Why do you exclude a nonhierarchical view of the world, or say it is not possible?

KRIER This change is in everybody's mind, but it does not allow anyone to fabricate a work of art, let alone to build a city or cultivate the countryside in a worthwhile manner. The new cosmology has not created anything worth dreaming about. The purpose of architecture is to make beautiful, solid, and comfortable buildings.

I am neither a doctor nor an analyst, but an architect and a legislator—a planner of cities. That is a very conservative occupation, in the same way that language is conservative. But compared to classical architecture, classical languages have deteriorated very little.

Classical languages communicate a limited set of similar—but not identical—ideas and phenomena. Each has a classical form, that is, a *best form*. For that very quality they should be conserved. But if there is very little poetry to be found, there is certainly no shortage of prose.

EISENMAN That is something very different. One reads the morning newspaper for the meaning of the words, the news; one then throws the paper away. On the other hand, when one reads Shakespeare one already knows the narrative; the play is read for the pleasure of the sensual nature of the words, their resonance.

Your theology is acceptable only because you are able to transform words into poetry through your drawings. Others may agree with you, but may not even be able to draw. This is the issue. Alberti put the question quite clearly. Anyone can learn to pull a bow back, but unless you know where to shoot the arrow it does not matter. But you could also argue that although you may know where to shoot the arrow, unless you can pull the bow back, the arrow may not land where you want. Two people could espouse the same theology and each could make a building, yet the buildings would not necessarily be equal. For example, Quinlan Terry does not make good buildings even though his theology is the same as yours. The same is true of Maurice Culot. His theology is similar, but his architecture is uninteresting. So the question arises: as an architect, is it better to be a poet with no theology or is it better to be a theologian with no poetry?

KRIER Quinlan Terry and Maurice Culot are among a very small number of friends I can trust almost blindly, whatever our differences in taste. In times of confusion we may all be invalids, but looking at our wounds is no cure. I do not overestimate the importance of philosophy, theology, or any kind of theoretical endeavor. They are useful crutches for invalids, but they are not goals in themselves.

A theory about eating is not necessary if you know how and what to eat. You would need such a theory only if one day people began to force food indiscriminately into any of their orifices.

EISENMAN I do not believe that Maurice Culot and Quinlan Terry are architects. They do nothing to transform material, that is, they do not transform language into any kind of art. Their work remains empty of poetics. They may be theologians, philosophers, social scientists, even cultural commentators—but they are not architects. Leon, what matters is that although you and Culot may say the same things, you can draw and he cannot.

KRIER No, Peter, and I do not see why you should want to applaud me at the expense of my friends. We are not talking here about subtleties, but about what is right and wrong. People must have a good command of language in order to speak properly; among those who do so, there are very few poets. Architects have first to learn the rules of their art before even thinking about being poets. The art of building is concerned with creating an environment that is pleasing to all our senses without being alienating to any one of them. Architecture is not about expressing existential anxiety or opinions of any kind.

EISENMAN But the history of great cities has always been about the expression of culture, not the making of "the good life." Architects of the eighteenth and nineteenth centuries did not think of themselves as making pleasing buildings so much as expressing a condition of man—or in contemporary terms, the zeitgeist.

KRIER Let us not discuss the zeitgeist. It is not our concern. The zeitgeist is there despite us; the more clever we think we are in dealing with it, the more stupid we may one day appear.

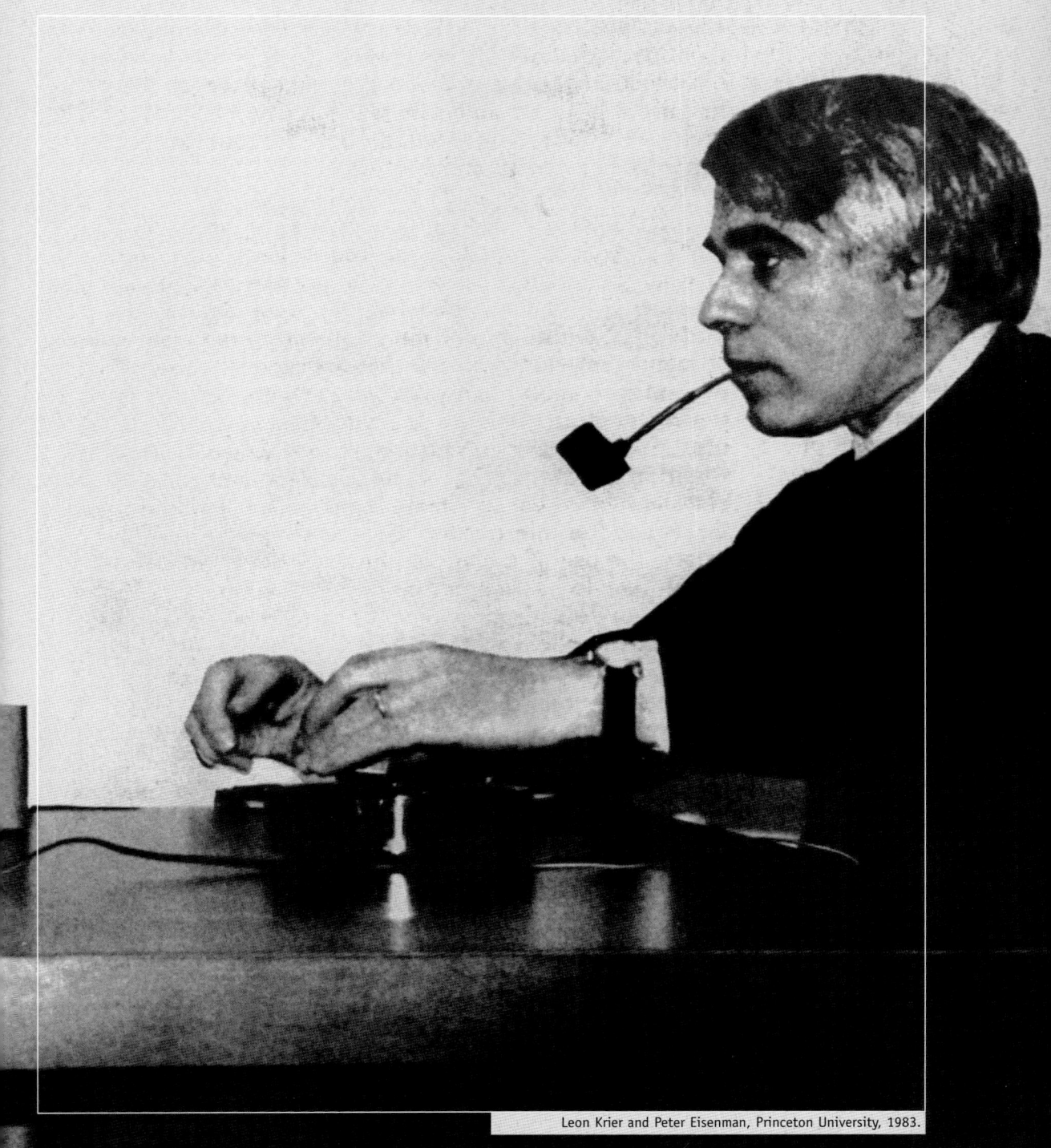
Leon Krier and Peter Eisenman, Princeton University, 1983.

EISENMAN You are right, the zeitgeist is none of our business. The difference between signification, representation, and replication is important. If one were to rebuild the Parthenon today in Charlottesville, it would be a replica of the Parthenon; it would not necessarily represent the spirit or the attitude of the Parthenon but merely reproduce the structure. If one were to build a building that was a transformation of the Parthenon but still contained recognizable symbolic imagery of the Parthenon, it would be an example of representation. One could also build a rectilinear building with formal characteristics integral to the Parthenon but without any representative qualities; it would signify something similar to that which the Parthenon signifies—that is, its inherent architectural relationships. Representation deals with expression and speaking, and signification deals with the innate structure of things that enables them to be spoken. I would like to argue that what Quinlan Terry does—at best—is represent, often replicate, and very rarely signify or concern himself with the nature of signification. An architect should take the classical, if you want, and then in some way transform it to address the problem of signification—because that is what architecture is about.

KRIER Your definitions make sense, but the issues you raise cannot be the obsessive concern of a classical architect who builds. Quinlan Terry, for example, is not involved with these questions, because he uses very accurately a language that had resolved all the problems of representation and signification long before he began to learn it.

EISENMAN Do you mean, therefore, that he is of no interest to theologians and vice versa?

KRIER For Quinlan Terry, the act of building has a symbolic dimension and a strong redeeming effect because even if he builds isolated structures, they are the bricks with which he is building a beautiful world. On top of that, he is using a system that has made its mark on cities and landscapes for two thousand years virtually without interruption. From that perspective, forty years of modern barbarism are a trifle. Indeed, there is no need to be as pessimistic as I am. My own maxim is "Everything or nothing, here and now and wherever I can see." That probably sounds rather fanatical—and it is. Nowadays I get extremely impatient with any kind of nonsense. I have to consider the city in its global cohesion, and if the legislation that rules the city is nonsensical, I feel that that is where I have to begin. Only in that way can the constant rebuilding, repairing, and rearranging of cities happen in an orderly and pleasing way.

But I would defend Quinlan Terry above and beyond all this, for he is virtually the only living architect in whose buildings I could live.

EISENMAN As a Jew and an "outsider," I have never felt a part of that "classical" world. I feel that modernism was the product of an alienated culture with no roots suddenly being brought into a bourgeois situation. In other words, modernists were suddenly out of the ghettos and in the cities. The philosophy that would abolish modernism proposes that if we return the world to the way it was before the alienated individuals took over, everything would be worked out. I am not convinced. When you say it is all worked out, I still feel like an outsider.

KRIER The problems of Jewish intellectuals are of no interest to architecture as a fine art.

EISENMAN Nevertheless, it is difficult for me to have a discussion with you when I hear you say it is all worked out.

KRIER Schinkel said that each epoch has its own expression in the fine arts. What is too often forgotten is what he went on to say, that progress had been so great in the fine arts in the past that it was virtually impossible to improve upon the system. Classical architecture as an artistic system has reached the typological and morphological perfection that the human species reached millions of years ago. Humanity continues to reproduce the same types of beings.

You will agree that however ancient that genetic system may be, it needs no improvement; any innovation in it is an aberration. At the same time, each human being is always a completely novel, unique, and irreproducible individual.

Our purpose as artists and architects is to understand the universal system and order that allows us to create objects of fine art just as nature creates *individuals*. That is what defines classicism: it is the fundamental system that allows us to create objects of *timeless* beauty.

EISENMAN Classicism is the representation of the idea of purity found in the natural world. As I said before, it is not possible today to represent the classical idea of purity—the harmony of man and nature—because biological and physical forces unleashed by man have destroyed that ideal condition. One can no longer use classical means for representation because what they represent no longer exists. All one can do is replicate classical forms; but they are significant of nothing.

KRIER The bomb carried in the human mind is much more dangerous than an actual one. To forbid good architecture because we live in terrible times is absurd.

EISENMAN I think a beautiful building is a modern building.

KRIER That is a contradiction in terms.

EISENMAN Who is to judge?

KRIER You!

EISENMAN Then there are no judges?

KRIER One must be one's own judge because other judges are unreliable.

EISENMAN But you once said that people who design modern buildings will probably burn in hell. You then become their judge.

KRIER Yes. Rather, they force others to live in their hell.

EISENMAN How can you know that? Who puts you in touch with those facts?

KRIER I just observe how and where architects live; they rarely live in their own buildings or in new towns. That is only a fine point.

EISENMAN Why is architecture about living in buildings? Building concerns shelter, construction, defying the laws of gravity, providing accommodation. Building can solve many functions—whether it is a building as an ocean liner, a building as a castle, or a building as a log cabin. A work of architecture is necessarily a building, but in itself a building is not a significant condition to define architecture. That is, since a building is not architecture, architecture must be something more than building, in the same way that literature is more than journalism. But if we would agree that people do not *need* to live in architecture but in buildings, then what is architecture if it is not a necessary part of living?

KRIER It is, obviously, not enough to have fine houses; a city also needs temples and monuments. Architecture is not concerned with the private realm. It shapes the public domain, the common world.

EISENMAN Would you agree that if we built a "public" wall, anything could be clipped on behind it?

KRIER Even if it becomes a public enterprise, housing is not a subject for "architecture"; it is not monumental. Twisted minds wanted housing to be the "monument of the twentieth century." But housing is the sum of private functions that even in great number become no more interesting when put on public display. There is nothing grand, ceremonious, or important about housing. That is why its monumentalization is always painfully boring, meaningless, and false.

EISENMAN Why not make a public facade, like a colonnade, for those private functions? For example, you would probably agree that the Ludwigstrasse is a pretty good street. Do you care what goes on behind the facades of the Ludwigstrasse?

KRIER Yes, very much so. The Ludwigstrasse is a beautiful but deadly place. You cannot take only one detail of the classical world and dispense with all the rest. You cannot have just beautiful facades with industrial nonsense going on behind them. In the classical world, just as in the natural world, each idea, each object, each creature has a place that is both sufficient and necessary. That, of course, does not exclude accidents, catastrophes, and illness.

EISENMAN You said that housing in the public realm is not important. You were saying that since private functions cannot have a public face, they have been reduced to anonymity.

KRIER The artistic and material means for sheltering private and public functions must of necessity be different. All the individual parts must add up to a harmonious whole, which is the city. This does not mean that even a modest structure should not be beautiful in its own way.

Today's fragments unfortunately do not add up to anything but an assemblage of spare parts, as Jaquelin Robertson puts it. These parts may in some cases be beautiful, but if you dismember a beautiful *individual*, for example, you will have a dead body—however ravishing its pieces may still be.

EISENMAN Since the French Revolution there have been no "beautiful" cities. Before the French Revolution, in a hierarchical society, someone was responsible for the public well-being. Today that public domain is characterized merely by the accumulation of private wellbeing and has nothing to do with the *res publica*. How do you reconcile the fact that a social revolution—to which you subscribe—unwittingly was compelled to destroy the beauty and order that you so cherish?

KRIER Revolutions are events of violent change. I would not subscribe to any such enterprise.

EISENMAN You would support the results of that social revolution.

KRIER I don't really see what good came of it. It was the start of two hundred years of industrial massacre of a moral and material kind. The grandeur of its moral ideas has faded terribly as a consequence. It is certainly pointless to regret the unavoidable, but then to applaud the inevitable is foolish and irresponsible.

It is interesting that authority has shifted from the universal and cultural to the material and industrial level. That shift has been lethal for the fine arts and for the moral foundations of artists' authority. Beyond that, artists have not only been bled of their authority but continue to sacrifice it whenever they can on the altars of industrial ideology. When architects gave up their historic role, their authority was absorbed by politicians and technicians. Those people have no interest and no capacity to promote architecture.

EISENMAN One of my primary concerns as an architect is to find out what architecture is. You at least seem certain of what architecture is—that its purpose is to create pleasurable environments. I would argue that that is the purpose of *building*. For me, architecture is the creation of significant environments that are more than merely pleasurable, more than what is necessary. In that way, the realm of architecture is totally useless in a utilitarian, industrial, and progressive sense. Then I would argue that representation and replication of these classical forms do not create significance. I would argue that since the role for the "Greek" temple no longer exists, the use of a classical order deriving from the Greek temple has nothing to do with signification and nothing to do with architecture. I would go so far as to say that it is the *only* thing that has nothing to do with architecture. Everything *except* what you stand for could be possible in architecture. Since your initial values—classical order—are associated with a function that no longer exists, you can only make a representation of that function. Until we find a system of signification related to the order of current symbolic needs, we will not have an architecture.

KRIER You are caught in art historical categories. The Greek temple is but one realization of the idea of the "temple."

EISENMAN It also refers to an idea of classical order.

KRIER Accumulation of capital is the highest purpose of industrial capitalism. All other human and natural values are subordinate to that role. Consequently, an abstract world is created full of abstract things, however paradoxical that may sound. However big that mountain of money may one day become, it will not, in fact, be more real but more and more abstract and valueless. In contrast, cultivation of the fine arts results in the accumulation of real and beautiful objects. Beautiful cities are literally concrete accumulations of human work inspired by moral ideas. Such beautiful objects and buildings are not only symbols and representations of values but are themselves moral values based on a universal plan.

EISENMAN Who is to say that a universal plan should take the form of the classical city? The Kantian idea of the thing in itself, the will to signify, has never had a preference for the classical. You will it to be so.

KRIER Again, you are using art historical qualifications. The classical idea does not belong to any one period. It is quite simply the idea of the *best possible*.

EISENMAN The best? It means a certain kind of order.

KRIER It means the *best possible*.

EISENMAN "Best" is not what we are talking about. Classical does not come with an a priori value judgment. Maybe good, maybe better, but not necessarily "best."

KRIER That is what it means. Classical is what belongs to the highest class, the highest form, the highest standard of excellence. There is no point in saying more.

EISENMAN There is also no best without worst; it is a relative term. The very nature of best means there must be disagreement about it. I am allowed, therefore, to disagree with the classical connotation of "best." If someone says to you that he is doing his best, although it may not be classical in a stylistic sense, and you say, "Well, I do not happen to like the style," then *you* are being the art historian.

KRIER Let me use an example. This object standing between us may fulfill the purpose of the table. It does not, however, withstand a critical glance for more than a second. Not only is it ugly, it is also quite uncomfortable: its edges, its surface, its legs are unpleasant to look at and to touch. A classical table, on the other hand, could be used and studied by a critical person for three thousand years without ever inspiring frustration as to its construction and appearance. Massimo Scolari has said that beautiful objects are the only friends that will never betray you. That is the best possible definition of the classical world.

EISENMAN He is one of the best architects I know. I think that you agree. Yet he does not do what you propose. His work, more than that of any other architect, seems to describe the new sensibility I am talking about. He is attempting to deal with the idea of imminent destruction. How do you feel about the seeming contradiction between your theology and his work?

KRIER Scolari's paintings are not projects of what he wants the world to be like. He is neither a monster nor a sadist, but as a poet he observes what could well be the unavoidable. His paintings are beautiful illustrations of a world in total disarray, beautiful and awe-inspiring illustrations of industrial devastation and exhaustion.

EISENMAN But I also think his paintings are architecture. They are images of the fact of an immanent present, that is, the future today—the present as end, not the future as end. As a statement his work comes closer to expressing what architecture is about—not *should be* about, but *is* about—than your work.

KRIER You may well be right, Peter, but so help us God.

History

No

Sarah Whiting

Those who seem to negate history produce historically motivated work, those who try not to cut their links with it, run into the shoals of ambiguity. [1]

It would be better, then, to accept reality as it really is and give the historian a dialectical role in respect to the architect, almost to the point of constant opposition. [2]

It is useless to propose purely architectural alternatives. The search for an alternative within the structures that condition the very character of architectural design is indeed an obvious contradiction of terms. [3]

Had Manfredo Tafuri been an adman, forced to reduce his turgid prose to catchy phrases, his success would have been more ideological than commercial; Nike would have been disappointed in him, but Nancy Reagan would have swooned, for Tafuri all but coined the negative impulse of architectural theory in the 1970s: "Just say no." *No*'s monosyllabic agency only negates (no is the *only* option), thereby offering an unambiguously simple formula for a seemingly difficult response, a reassuringly dialectical opposition. This twenty-fifth anniversary of the Eisenman-Krier debate—in itself, a dialectical opposition of two practitioners who each initially forged a practice out of the negative—offers an opportune moment for inquiring after the health, even the life span, of our inherited propensity for the negative. Simply put, when does no negate itself?

The mistaken perception of no's simplicity and singularity obscures the complexity underlying Tafuri's stance, a complexity that reveals itself only through a slow reading of his difficult textual tapestry, which weaves together history, theory, and criticism. The Cliffs Notes conclusion hastily drawn around Tafuri is that architecture has only two options, each a shade of no: succumb to capitalism's instrumentality or retreat into silence. Either choice amounts to what, as K. Michael Hays has noted, has been called Tafuri's "assisted suicide" vis-à-vis architecture, the smoking gun being Tafuri's 1969 essay "Toward a Critique of Architectural Ideology."[4]

The title of the subsequent book version of this killer article—*Architecture and Utopia: Design and Capitalist Development*—only begins to reveal the host of multiple dialectical oppositions that underlie Tafuri's intellectual strategy, here and in his other writings. For Tafuri, *and* is not a Venturi-esque conjunction of addition or juxtaposition but a self-destructive, hermetic pairing, a coupling mechanism whose impossibility (as Tafuri demonstrates) ultimately nullifies its very existence. Joined together, architecture and utopia suffocate. "It is useless to struggle," Tafuri concludes, "when one is trapped inside a capsule with no exit."[5]

This sci-fi image of a Sartrean *huis clos* formalism seals the fate of the practicing architect who may aspire to a social-political good but who can never reconcile those aspirations with the tools that modernism has left him: the *objets trouvés* of the avant-garde's forms, slogans, and technologies. According to Tafuri, the practicing architect's no is not a critical or operational no but rather a compulsory no, as in "no choice," "no matter," "no exit." Even modernism's most successful efforts to effect ideological change through form (the expressionists) or through program (the Bauhaus, the constructivists) were ultimately doomed, for they were "critique[s] made from a rearguard position that is therefore incapable, by its very nature, of proposing universal alternatives."[6] Tafuri saw architecture's "return to language [as] a proof of failure," a failure imposed by consumer capitalism's ruthless, steady elimination of all other possibilities. Only a "restructuring of production and consumption in general; in other words, the planned coordination of production"[7] might bring architecture forward from the rear guard, but architects, especially those of the avant-garde, were unlikely ever to accept that they might gain effectiveness only by backseating themselves to the planner.

Although Tafuri silences the practice of architecture, he offers a ready voice to architecture's history and criticism, turning no, or the negative, into a form of critical textual project, all the while limiting the projective possibilities of architectural practice. Criticism and history are practices that repackage the past and, despite Tafuri's famous exhortations against operative criticism, simultaneously whisper the hint of a future for practice.[8] Though privileged, criticism and history remain strategically fuzzy in Tafuri's oeuvre: by skipping across decades, movements, writers, and practitioners with dizzying speed—if it's page 124, it must be Paul Rudolph . . . *and* Peter Behrens *and* William Morris *and* the Five *and, and, and* . . .[9] —Tafuri leaves the reader flushed from the race but not quite certain which track has been run. Toward the conclusion of *Theories and History*, he offers seemingly precise roles for the historian and the critic, which in turn offer some guidance to architecture:

> *The historian accentuates the contradictions of history and offers them crudely, in their reality, to those whose responsibility it is to create new formal worlds. But at the same time, history and criticism set a limit to ambiguity in architecture. By leading the works back into more general contexts, and in the very moment that it hypothesises an historical role for them, criticism delimits a field of values within which it is possible to attribute unequivocal meanings to architecture.*[10]

But the limiting of ambiguity and the attribution of the unequivocal are like the elusive merry-go-round's golden ring: how, *how*, does one hone in on these limits, these definitions? Eight pages later, in the book's final paragraph, Tafuri throws cold water on the eager reader, who by this time is pathetically desperate to claim the prize after going round and round through so many pages: "Solutions are not to be found in history." Tafuri then softens his brutal blow, though only slightly, by acknowledging that "the only possible way [the *only*!] is the exasperation of the antitheses, the frontal clash of the positions, and the accentuation of contradictions. And this not for a particular form of sado-masochism," he adds (unconvincingly), "but in the hypothesis of a radical change that will leave behind both the anguished present situation and the temporary tasks we have tried to make clear to ourselves . . ." The going is tough, but you're left with a sliver of hope: *hypothesis* and *radical change* are both singular, suggesting a potentially positive conclusion way out on the far, far horizon.

This seemingly requisite pairing of pessimism and optimism is the one and that does not self-destruct in Tafuri but rather holds out a glimmer of hope. It's also an and that recurs again and again in some form or another throughout Tafuri's writing: the bitter aftertaste of pessimism souring a gluttonous trail of theoretical or historical bonbons; the saccharine suggestion of optimism sweetening an acrid historical excursus. It's a pairing that keeps the easy answer in check, that keeps total despair from suffocating the reader, that offers some agency within the world of architecture, although the complexities underlying his textual practice obscure whether that agency extends much beyond Tafuri himself.

For that agency is cast in the arresting but ambiguous role of an "angel with dirty hands."[11] Surely referencing the hapless angel of Walter Benjamin's "Theses on the Philosophy of History," who is powerless to do anything but describe the ever expanding debris of history at his feet, Tafuri's angel is implicated in his own despair; he cannot avoid engaging capitalism's processes of production. Unlike the architect, who cannot overcome those processes, who can only be silenced by them, Tafuri's sullied angels of history (which, one would assume, include Tafuri himself) possess some ability to act: "Historical criticism," he claims, "must know how to balance on the razor's edge that separates detachment from participation."[12] The image of the razor's edge is only one of a series of images of death, destruction, and violence that in various forms punctuate Tafuri's texts. This razor implies a precarious—even impossible—balancing act, an unstable fulcrum across which historical precision and contemporary repercussion can find only a tentative relationship. That relationship is, strangely enough, described in terms of design. The historian's first task is to historicize—that is, to identify and contextualize—history's fragments, and then to compose them, effectively redesigning history: the critical act will consist of a recomposition of the fragments once they are historicized, that is, in their "remontage."[13]

Tafuri's nihilism vis-à-vis architectural practice most closely resembles the negative thinking of his younger colleague at the Istituto di Storia dell'Architettura in Venice, philosopher Massimo Cacciari, who believes that the monetary economy of capitalism evacuates the inner bounds of the self, precluding the possibility of any form of subjectivity.[14] Building upon his analysis of Georg Simmel's writings on the modern metropolis, Cacciari developed his theory of negative thought as an alternative to dialectics. Nihilism avoids the false positivism of the synthesis by bringing to an end "the very idea of solution." Like Tafuri, Cacciari sees nihilism as revealing capitalism's ideological stronghold, its ratio, "the eminently productive ratio of technique and its power of control, manipulation, and foresight."[15]

While this form of nihilism is possible within architecture (Cacciari offers Adolf Loos as an example), it works best as a practice in the realm of criticism. As Patrizia Lombardo notes in her extended introduction to Cacciari's *Architecture and Nihilism*, "The trajectory of the theory of the Metropolis brings negative thought to the mode of commentary, mystically—not philosophically—conceived as a plunge into the limits of language."[16] Understood in this light, nihilism is like Tafuri's "remontage" of history. Nihilism multiplies outward, illustrating the impossibility of a single conclusion or synthesis: "Fulfillment [of nihilism] implies neither the task of effecting solution nor that of effecting the end of all solution [sic], but the idea of composition as a listening to the differences, as an acknowledgement of their characteristic and as the comprehensible communication of this characteristic."[17] Difference, multiplicity, plurality: these terms form the foundation of the critical theory that spanned the twenty years from the late 1960s through the 1980s. Messier than negative dialectics, Cacciari's nihilism and Tafuri's no are critical tools reflecting their own time.[18] At the same time, they are attempts to come to terms with how to draw something out of modernism's avant-garde moment without either idealizing its utopian premise or capitulating to its capitalist counterpart.

But where do they leave you, other than in the midst of a tentative construct, born of fragments and destined to coalesce those fragments only in the most passive of ways, as a historical response? At this point, it is almost impossible to avoid hearing Nietzsche's warning: "Now picture yourself the historical virtuoso of the present day . . . He has become a passive sounding-board whose reflected tones act upon other similar sounding-boards: until at last the whole air of an age is filled with the confused humming of these tender and kindred echoes."[19] To return to a question posed at the beginning of this paper, when does no negate itself? When does it become a mere echo chamber of historical noise? For Nietzsche, the historian's recomposition of fragments is rendered instrumental in that it has an effect, a result rather than a mere illustration of ineffectuality; it doesn't just reveal, it acts. For Nietzsche, critical history (as opposed to monumental history or antiquarian history) is a judging of the past:

> *If he is to live, man must possess and from time to time employ the strength to break up and dissolve a part of the past: he does this by bringing it before the tribunal, scrupulously examining it and finally condemning it . . . It is always a dangerous process, especially so for life itself: and men and ages which serve life by judging and destroying a past are always dangerous and endangered men and ages . . . If we condemn these aberrations and regard ourselves as free of them, this does not alter the fact that we originate in them.*[20]

The effect of critical history, then, is this public act of exposure whereby exposure is combined with condemnation. So the agency of the critical lies in its negative: its vociferous condemnation of a historical moment. Has the nihilism ushered in by Tafuri become an endless trial—the ineffectual but ever expanding dustbin of architecture culture?

By 1987, when *Modern Architecture* and *The Sphere and the Labyrinth* were translated into English and published in the United States, Tafuri's historical condemnation of architecture had rained down like a kind of radioactive critical fallout for almost twenty years. The contaminated results lay everywhere, filled every crevice, and proved their tenacity with their extraordinarily long half-life.

The architectural practices of both Peter Eisenman and Leon Krier emerged during this period of critical (radio)activity. Writing with Francesco Dal Co, Tafuri returns to the angel of history when addressing these two architects' work as well as that of other practices constituting "The Experience of the Seventies," the final chapter of Tafuri and Dal Co's architectural survey: "Architecture seeks to recast in contemporary phrases the meanings destroyed by the fury of the Angelus Novus, as reinterpreted by Walter Benjamin. The gap dividing such attempts from the reality of the relations of production appears unbridgeable. The return to poetry inexorably cuts the umbilical cord that tied the avant-garde to the real."[21] While Tafuri and Dal Co conclude with the dubious compliment that the work of this final chapter represents "a condition of intellectual labor that suggests certain final reflections," their descriptions of the practices in question reveal their belief that such reflections hardly glitter in a future, outward orientation but instead mark the end of previous, historical projects:

> *The archaeologizing of Stirling, the nostalgia of Kahn, the irony of Venturi have much to do with the approaches being tried now by the most promising among the architects too young to have been involved in what is still called the modern movement. Without Stirling, the reined designs of the brothers Leon and Robert Krier would be inexplicable. Like Sir Arthur John Evans, the English archaeologist who recreated the lost world of ancient Crete in his own manner, the Kriers make pleasant play with the bits of the past dug up by Stirling. But, as was also the case in the reconstructed Crete, in their architectural jigsaw puzzles the really original pieces are rare . . .*

> Likewise, without Venturi one could not make sense of the multiple formal games that so-called radical American groups, spoiled by the very generous "social salary" that the American system grants to the potentially unemployed, propose for the enjoyment of a restricted public of adepts... The game nevertheless has its risks... Look too at the ascetic abstractionism of Peter Eisenman; his exasperated formalism seeks to pin down the perennial logic of the architectural signs and ends up by discovering that all that can be done in such an operation is to train a spotlight on the alienated state of those signs.[22]

After reading such eloquent but backhanded compliments, the reader is left convinced that Krier's and Eisenman's strategies are squarely situated within the airless vacuum of Tafuri's no-fly zone. Indeed, both Eisenman and Krier have long operated under a Tafuri-like mantle of negativity, although their particular negativities differ greatly and each has subsequently evolved in very different directions. Krier's endless pursuit has been to condemn modernism's culture of invention, innovation, and discovery; Eisenman's aim, on the other hand, has been to condemn the stranglehold that norms and conventions have imposed upon the possibilities of invention, innovation, and discovery.

Despite their differences, both Krier and Eisenman have relied upon some form of negative strategy to construct their condemnations, especially in their early careers. Perhaps the most famous negative of all is Krier's oft-quoted proclamation "I am an architect because I do not build." With this statement Krier directly echoes Tafuri, concluding that nothing can be done within the existing processes of capitalist production. Rather than retreat to the realm of a mute architecture that ultimately cannot but confirm capitalism's crass cultural compromise, Krier opts for absolute silence. When the Prince of Wales's patronage eventually offered him an opportunity to build as he wanted, outside capitalism's constraints, Krier chose a different kind of negativity, that of the negative dialectic.[23] Krier's cartoon-sketches of contemporary architectural problems are almost always presented in dialectical terms: the binaries consist of extreme opposites frequently resolved in a Krierian vision of a possible, desirable third. A "Derelict Modernist Masterpiece" is contrasted with "Conservative Restoration (Nostalgic)," which restores the masterpiece to its early modern state; whereas the synthesis between these two extremes that Krier advocates is "Creative (Forward Looking) Restoration," which is, essentially, a complete makeover of the derelict modernist box into a classical villa. Unlike Cacciari's nihilism, Krier's no is always dialectical, at the service of a synthesis, which, for Krier, is always a classical vernacular one. Not only does this synthesis fall into the category of "solution" that Cacciari warns against—decrying the stasis that such false "fulfillment" would engender—but it also obstructs the very criticality that Tafuri wishes upon the act of "remontage."[24] If remontage is restorative rather than critical, it will (as demonstrated in Krier's village design for Poundbury) render history's fragments whole again, erasing their fissures, fractures, and fragmentations. The negativity of Krier's practice, then, is neither critical nor productive in the sense of producing either a new vision for the future or a new reading of the past. Tafuri would point to Krier's classical-vernacular idyll as constituting one of the "impotent and ineffectual myths" that he decries in *Architecture and Utopia*. For Krier, it is that very myth that constitutes architecture: looking backward offers the only possible resistance to capitalism's technocracy.

Eisenman's negative critique, on the other hand, more closely resembles Tafuri's own textual practice of critical remontage, without succumbing to the literalist Tafurism of Krier's silent nonpractice or the false synthesis of a restorative practice. Eisenman nests historical binaries (classical versus modern), formal binaries (walls versus columns), ideological binaries (presentness versus absence), and disciplinary binaries (landscape versus architecture) in an expansive, kaleidoscopic strategy that is simultaneously architectural and textual and where synthesis is never possible, and certainly not desirable. While Tafuri and Dal Co's reading of Eisenman's houses rings true—the accomplishment of these houses is indeed to "train a spotlight on the alienated state of [architectural] signs"—it is unclear why the two historians find that accomplishment wanting. Finding the limit of architectural language is not that different from Tafuri's own project of revealing the limits of architecture's critique.

For Eisenman, no is an oppositional strategy rather than a mute one. Eisenman's goal was (and continues to be) to distill the structure of architecture's form in an effort to find meaning established by, as opposed to associated with, architecture. In the house projects, architecture's semantic readings do not disappear at the limit; instead, they are thrown into complex relationships—layered, oscillating, and composite—with one another. The oppositional red and green stairs in House VI, for example, offer culturally established, immediate semantic readings of stop and go: the red, upside-down stair, which cannot be ascended, says "stop," while the functional green stair, leading up to the second floor, indicates "go." But a conceptual reading of the two colors interferes with an iconic one: red and green combine to make gray. Eisenman's choice of these two colors was a deliberate effort to tangle color's symbolic value with its purely indexical use by literally graying it out.[25]

Where his ambition differs from modernism is that Eisenman's subject *and* object emerge from formal manipulations; neither one is conclusive or singular. In other words, while the modernist project was meant to form a particular subject, Eisenman is more intent on transforming subjectivity, inciting possibilities without predicting them. Eisenman started with the modernist project of estrangement but quickly expanded his scope to a project of engagement. His "cities of artificial excavation" projects—Cannaregio, Berlin, Long Beach, La Villette, and the Wexner Center—evenly arrayed historical and fictional information about a project's site, history, and context, permitting subjects to rearrange that information as they wanted. The subject was engaged in writing the project's narrative, its remontage, assembling it from the material provided. This strategy was modern in its desire to use architecture to affect a subject, and postmodern in its flattening out of source material, rendering all "origins" equal and hence simultaneously valuable and suspect.

Just as the excavation projects springboarded from estrangement to engagement, Eisenman's more recent work has further accelerated his desire to continually embed potential in architecture. As he has begun to build larger, more complex projects, the strategies of estrangement and engagement have been joined by attention to a visceral and even programmatic entanglement of subject and object. The Aronoff Center for Design and Art at the University of Cincinnati offers a series of echoing architectural figures that multiply, amplify, and reorder views, frustrating and even reversing the simultaneously controlling and open-ended viewpoints of the project's axes. These vertical and horizontal cross-views consistently interrupt the school's symbolic shared space, rendering that space ambiguous; they suggest unforeseen programmatic relationships among the building's varied constituencies of students, faculty, and administration. The result is unnerving: what ought to be the apex of spatial synthesis becomes a sequence of visual antigravities that untethers expected behaviors.

What Eisenman started with the Aronoff Center, he has almost infinitely multiplied in the more-than-750,000-square-foot project under construction for the City of Culture of Galicia in Spain. The City of Culture will become a new pilgrimage destination in Santiago de Compostela, transforming subjects not through religion but through a remontage that plays architecture, landscape, and urbanism off one another: the hilltop site has been both carved and extracted, making it nearly impossible to tell where landscape ends and building starts. Spaces between and within buildings are rendered similarly ambiguous, making it possible to redefine programs typically associated with either interiors or exteriors. The possibilities of transformation are the point of any pilgrimage site, but change does not come easily: at Santiago, just like at the Aronoff and in all of Eisenman's projects, those subjected to this architecture will never experience the luxury of being passive. Instead, they will be snared in an atmosphere of calculated estrangement whose vertiginous, agitating, and even frustrating qualities are laced with the ever hopeful opiate of transformation. No mere project of detached abstraction, the remontage that comes with the collapse of the subject and the object into one another belies an almost euphoric optimism about architecture's possibilities.

It is Tafuri's strategy of negative critique as a historical enterprise that has exhausted itself, that is dead, but its use as a form of practice by Krier and Eisenman forms the springboard for a new stage of critical approach. Tafuri correctly points to architectural, and even intellectual, ineffectuality in the face of capitalism's hegemony. In making this the criteria for judgment, Tafuri necessarily kills architecture. Once it has become a corpse, frozen in place, all that is left for us to do, either as practitioners or as historians, is to examine it, perform an autopsy, and try to reveal the impasse that led to its critical demise. Given the pervasive nature of global capitalism today, the possibility of resurrecting architecture when it is defined in this manner is ever more remote.

Because they are architects, both Krier and Eisenman necessarily treat architecture's body not as something to expose and examine, like the corpse under Dr. Tulp's knife in Rembrandt's famous painting, but as something *live* on which they need to work, like Benjamin's surgeon. That is how Krier and Eisenman move beyond Tafuri's impasse. In other words, while an autopsy demands examination, exposure, and judgment, surgery demands analysis, dissection, *and* a hopeful ambition to construct life. Both Krier and Eisenman achieve this turn by reclaiming the possibility, even the necessity, of utopia for architecture.

In projecting specifically architectural rather than complete social utopias, Krier and Eisenman reclaim a potential territory of expertise for the architect and for architectural history. The shift from a social to an architectural utopia is not a sellout to capitalism, as some critics might claim, but a means of positing where architecture's political effect might find some traction. Krier's utopia is a world where premodern architectural ideals succeed in maintaining the moral underpinnings of the present and future. Eisenman's utopia is a world where architecture is able to maintain its autonomous definition and progression in the face of interdisciplinary threats. Both utopias have political reverberations, and both, like all utopias, necessarily require the negative as a means of part of their definition. (Even if Krier offers a vision of aesthetic order, he does so as a means of laying the groundwork for a socialist vision of individual autonomy within that order; Eisenman's aesthetic vision avoids social control in a more revolutionary manner, that is, through challenge to any form of order.)

For Tafuri, utopia as a project was precisely that which was impossible. No as a no-no (as a *don't do*) loomed larger than the utopian no. Utopia, even with the no that lies within its very definition, is arguably the world's biggest yes. Replacing "just say no" with "just do it" would be just another neutralizing strategy of dialectical opposition; in order to capitalize on utopia's possibilities rather than capitulate to capitalism's potential closing down of possibilities, no needs to be replaced with *ambition*, even if that ambition requires donning a potentially illusory utopian mantle.

1. Manfredo Tafuri, *Theories and History of Architecture* (1976; English trans., London: Granada, 1980), 39.

2. Tafuri, *Theories and History*, 64.

3. Manfredo Tafuri, *Architecture and Utopia: Design and Capitalist Development* (1973; English trans., Cambridge, Mass.: MIT Press, 1987), 181.

4. K. Michael Hays, "Tafuri's Ghost," in *ANY* 25–26: 36. Tafuri's "Toward a Critique of Architectural Ideology" was originally published in *Contropiano* 1 (January–April 1969).

5. Manfredo Tafuri, "Toward a Critique of Architectural Ideology" (1969), in *Architecture Theory since 1968*, ed. K. Michael Hays (New York: Rizzoli/Columbia Books on Architecture, 1998), 32.

6. Tafuri, "Toward a Critique," 23.

7. Tafuri, *Architecture and Utopia*, 100.

8. For an excellent discussion of Tafuri's own operative criticism, see Mark Wigley, "Post-Operative History," *ANY* 25–26: 47–53.

9. Tafuri, *Theories and History*, 124.

10. Tafuri, *Theories and History*, 229.

11. Manfredo Tafuri, "L'architecture dans le boudoir," in *The Sphere and the Labyrinth: Avant-Gardes and Architecture from Piranesi to the 1970s*, trans. Pellegrino d'Acierno and Robert Connolly (Cambridge, Mass.: MIT Press, 1987), 289.

12. Tafuri, "Introduction," *Sphere and the Labyrinth*, 11.

13. Tafuri, "The Historical Project," *Sphere and the Labyrinth*, 15.

14. Massimo Cacciari, *Architecture and Nihilism: On the Philosophy of Modern Architecture*, trans. Stephen Sartarelli (New Haven: Yale University Press, 1993). Outside of architecture circles, Cacciari might be best known as the mayor of Venice who married Woody Allen and Soon-Yi Previn in 1997 (an extreme form of nihilist practice?).

Regarding Cacciari's nihilism, see also Tomas Llorens, "Manfredo Tafuri: Neo-Avant-Garde and History," in Demetri Porphyrios, *Architectural Design: On the Methodology of Architectural History*, special issue (1981): 83–95; and Hilde Heynen, *Architecture and Modernity: A Critique* (Cambridge, Mass.: MIT Press, 1999), especially "The Venice School, or the Diagnosis of Negative Thought," 128–47.

15. Cacciari, *Architecture and Nihilism*, 201.

16. Patrizia Lombardo, "Introduction: The Philosophy of the City," in Cacciari, *Architecture and Nihilism*, liii.

17. Cacciari, *Architecture and Nihilism*, 209.

18. Jacques Derrida's *Writing and Difference* and *On Grammatology* were both originally published in 1967; in 1977, Cacciari published an essay on multiplicity, difference, and transformation in the work of Michel Foucault and Gilles Deleuze: "Il problema del politico in Deleuze e Foucault," in *Il Dispositivo Foucault*, ed. Franco Rella and Georges Teyssot (Venice: Cluva, 1977).

19. Friedrich Nietzsche, *Untimely Meditations*, trans. R. J. Hollingdale (Cambridge: Cambridge University Press, 1983), 90.

20. Nietzsche, *Untimely Meditations*, 75–76.

21. Manfredo Tafuri and Francesco Dal Co, *Modern Architecture*, vol. 2 (1976; English trans., New York: Rizzoli, 1987), 390–92.

22. Tafuri and Dal Co, *Modern Architecture*, vol. 2, 384–87.

23. Prince Charles hired Krier as his architectural consultant in 1988, a collaboration that resulted in the design of Poundbury, a traditional town in Dorset, England.

24. See especially Cacciari's epilogue.

25. Peter Eisenman, conversation with the author, May 30, 2003.

"Colin Rowe"

Anthony Vidler

I have been asked to speak on the subject of "Colin Rowe": an ambiguous assignment in the best of cases, hovering between Colin Rowe as personal subject and intellectual object. It appears even more ambiguous in the context of this symposium, set up, so to speak, as a contest between two apparently opposite but in reality closely related architectural positions, the radical formalism of the conservative avant-garde and the radical formalism of the conservative rear-guard, a symposium itself suspended between the personal and the political and framed around the equally ambiguous opposition between two other subjects/objects, "Leon Krier" and "Peter Eisenman," who have had ambiguous personal relationships with each other and with Colin Rowe, and even more ambiguous intellectual relations between themselves and Colin Rowe.

I begin with an apparently unambiguous citation of a citation:

There are two causes of beauty—natural and customary. Natural is from geometry consisting in uniformity, that is, equality and proportion. Customary beauty is begotten by the use, as familiarity breeds a love for things not in themselves lovely.[1]

These words are attributed to Christopher Wren and were published in his posthumous fragments, *Parentalia*, in the mid-eighteenth century. They are also cited by Colin Rowe as an epigraph to his 1947 article "The Mathematics of the Ideal Villa," where they were used to set up a discussion of the comparative uses of geometry and associative form in Palladio and Le Corbusier.

Wren's distinction might also, at least at first glance, seem appropriate in the context of the not-so-hidden intellectual agenda behind this symposium. For the implied opposition between the representative positions "Eisenman" and "Krier" might be equally characterized as that between a radical "autonomous" architecture internally considered to derive its formal condition as architecture from geometry, whether typological or topological, and an architecture deriving its authority from an evaluation of its social and cultural symbolism. In purely visual terms, this opposition manifests itself as one between abstract and realist; in historical terms, it might be seen as between an architecture that ostensibly extends the abstract formalism of the 1920s avant-gardes and one that returns to a restatement of the literal forms of classical tradition. On an ideological plane, we might say it stands as a contest between posthumanist modernism and retrohumanist postmodernism, between an assumption of a humanist subjectivity disseminated and perhaps irrevocably lost and one precariously surviving, perhaps to be regained.

It has been generally assumed, based on the testimony of Reyner Banham and Charles Jencks, that Rowe took sides in this debate; that in giving "the younger generation of architects the metaphor of the past, of history, of references, as a viable generator of present form" (Jencks), Rowe was "the true founder of postmodernist thinking in the field" (Banham).[2] Jencks's remarks are displayed prominently on the jacket of *The Mathematics of the Ideal Villa and Other Essays*, and the testimony of a follower, Alexander Caragonne, on the dust cover of *As I Was Saying*, a collection of Rowe's writings, is equally explicit. He characterizes Rowe as important for his questioning of "the eternal verities of modern architecture as propounded by the giants of the early twentieth century."[3] All of this has led to the conclusion, easy enough to confirm by a hasty reading of the essay titles and some of his students' work, that Rowe was in some way an antimodern, quasinostalgic humanist, dedicated to Biedermeier values and neoclassic form—which would put him perhaps more on the side of "Krier" than of "Eisenman."

A closer reading of Rowe's early essays, at least those written up to 1960—the year that marks the beginning of his friendship with Eisenman at Cambridge—might reveal not so much an antimodernist as an impassioned observer of the modern in the light of the past, a believer in the irrevocable advent of modernity and even in the existence of a modern zeitgeist. Certainly his analytical dissections of Le Corbusier and Mies van der Rohe, which have formed the approach of generations of scholars and architects, and his very willingness to introduce the work of the Five Architects indicate a sensibility not entirely adverse to certain versions of modern architecture. At the very least, this would signal an attraction to Eisenman equal to that to Krier.

This ambivalence is confirmed when we look at what Rowe actually wrote on the subject of Eisenman and Krier. We are left with no clear sense of critical authorization for one side or the other, of the kind offered by, for example, Sigfried Giedion in support of Le Corbusier or, alternatively, by Nikolaus Pevsner in support of Gropius; no hint of that "instrumental" criticism so castigated by Manfredo Tafuri as implicating the critic in the practice of the architect. Indeed, while at one point Tafuri was keen to engage the American Five, and certainly registered the impact of Aldo Rossi's neorationalist typology on Krier and others, albeit in a fundamentally critical vein, Rowe seems to have wanted to escape from any firm judgment on the issues raised. The better part of his introduction to *Five Architects* (1972) is taken up more with an autopsy of modern architecture's failure in the face of its ubiquitous success than with any extended discussion of the contents of the book. The burden of the argument rests on the disappearance of the moral and utopian impetus in European modernism, the seemingly nonideological modern architecture of the United States, and the opening left for the recuperation of historical "meaning" through the resurrection and extension of modernist codes. In Rowe's words, Eisenman "seems to have received a revelation in Como; Hejduk seems to wish affiliation both to synthetic Cubist Paris and Constructivist Moscow," and Graves, Gwathmey, and Meier have an "obviously Corbusian orientation." His conclusion, that the argument posed by the Five was "largely about the physique of building and only indirectly about its morale," avoided any confrontation with the nature of this new formalism qua architecture as meaningful language.[4] In the two-paragraph erratum slip to the 1975 reprint, Rowe vouchsafes little more in the way of appreciation than an extremely contorted assessment of the "bourgeois," "cosmopolitan erudition," and "belligerently second hand" character of the work. Its only merit, apparently, resides in the fact that "it is what *some* people and *some* architects want" and thus was difficult to fault, in principle at least.[5]

Krier, for his part, while gaining Rowe's notice in the early 1980s, fares little better in the context of Rowe's general support of historical typological investigation:

> How to react to that spectacle of semiotic argument, circular courtyards, neo-Grec peristyles, high staccato, Fellini billowing curtains, semi-Tuscan altane, the pseudo-Boullée, the neo-Schinkel, the revived Von Klenze, and all the other current, and "metaphysical," graphic paraphernalia? That the visuals are too easy and the apologetics too opaque?[6]

Rowe's conclusion was incisive: Krier's work was anti-programmatic (thus welcome), but his architectural practice consisted "of engaging schematic ideality" (thus typical) and was in any event produced by stencils (and was thereby inadequate to solve the problems of city and architecture).

Thus any easy assumption of oppositions emerges as caricature at best and wrong at worst. For a close examination of the writings in which Rowe worked out his critical position toward the difficulties and ambiguities inherent in Wren's (and Renaissance humanism's and the modern movement's) division of the world of form between "geometrical" and "customary" reveals not only a clearly distinct third term—"Rowe" as opposed to both "Eisenman" and "Krier"—but an interpretation of the modern movement and its relationships to the classical tradition that would in itself foreclose any such easy distinctions.

That the immediate postwar period, especially in England, saw a revival of interest in what was then called a New Palladianism is now a commonplace of intellectual history—indeed, it was a phenomenon that was almost immediately historicized. In his 1955 article "The New Brutalism," Banham pointed not only to the prevailing tendency for naming movements along the lines of art historical styles ("the New Empiricism," "the New Humanism," "the New Brutalism") but also to the then recent interest in Palladio and Palladianism, stimulated by the work of Rudolf Wittkower, whose *Architectural Principles in the Age of Humanism*, published in 1949, had explicitly informed the Smithsons' entry for the Coventry Cathedral Competition:

> One can safely posit the interference of historical studies again, for, though the exact priority of date as between the Smithsons' design and the publication of Professor Wittkower's Architectural Principles of [sic] the Age of Humanism is disputed (by the Smithsons) it cannot be denied that they were in touch with Wittkowerian studies at the time, and were as excited by them as anybody else.
>
> The general impact of Professor Wittkower's book on a whole generation of post-war architectural students is one of the phenomena of our time. Its exposition of a body of architectural theory in which function and form were significantly linked by the objective laws governing the Cosmos (as Alberti and Palladio understood them) suddenly offered a way out of the doldrum of routine-functionalist abdications, and neo-Palladianism became the order of the day. The effect of Architectural Principles has made it by far the most important contribution—for evil as well as good—by any historian to English architecture since Pioneers of the Modern Movement, and it precipitated a nice disputation on the proper uses of history. The question became: Humanist principles to be followed? or Humanist principles as an example of the kind of principles to look for? Many students opted for the former alternative, and Routine-Palladians soon became as thick on the ground as Routine-Functionalists. The Brutalists, observing the inherent risk of a return to pure academicism—more pronounced at Liverpool than at the AA—sheered off abruptly in the other direction and were soon involved in the organization of Parallel of Life and Art.[7]

In 1955, Banham was well aware that any "Palladianism" in British modern architecture had already been cast aside. He cited Peter Smithson's introduction of the "Parallel of Life and Art" exhibition to an Architectural Association student debate—"We are not going to talk about proportion and symmetry"—as the architect's "declaration of war on the inherent academicism of the neo-Palladians" and "crypto-academicism" in general.

Indeed, Banham had a similar purpose as he worked to identify a new "aformalism" emerging in the Hunstanton School, Sheffield University, and Golden Lane as taking over from the "formalism" of Palladian reference—a move, as we shall see, implicitly staged from a modernist/structuralist "typology" to a new, modernist, visual "topology."[8]

The historicization of the New Palladianism had in fact been accomplished the year before in a debate at the Royal Institute of British Architects around the motion "that systems of proportion make good design easier and bad design more difficult." Nikolaus Pevsner's defense of the motion had been countered by Misha Black and Peter Smithson himself. Smithson allowed that the issue "was important to architects as a matter of tooth and claw debate, in 1948 and 1949," when Palladian buildings were understood as "something to believe in . . . something that stood above what they were doing themselves." But in 1954 the issue was already "passé": "The right time for the Palladian revival was 1948." All the rest was no more than an "academic post-mortem" of the European postwar impulse, "as is also this debate at the RIBA."[9]

Peter Smithson's declaration of 1948 as the high point of Palladianism is interesting, because the often cited source of such principled Palladianism, Wittkower's *Architectural Principles in the Age of Humanism*, was not published until 1949, and this for the most part (if we believe the reviews) to a decidedly indifferent audience. Certainly the book was read by a group of young architects, including the Smithsons, Alan Colquhoun, Banham, and Rowe. The Smithsons wrote in protest against A. G. Butler's negative review in the *Architectural Review* (he had found it "exhausting," "unintelligible," and "almost a bore"[10]): "Dr. Wittkower is regarded by the younger architects as the *only* art historian working in England capable of describing and analyzing buildings in spatial and plastic terms and not in terms of derivation and dates." For the Smithsons, *Architectural Principles* was "the most important work on architecture published in England since the War."[11]

Smithson was writing here long after 1948. The central essay of Wittkower's book, "Principles of Palladio's Architecture," had been published in the *Journal of the Warburg and Courtauld Institutes* in two parts in 1944 and 1945, but this was hardly a source to be readily absorbed by the architectural community in London. Rather, we should look for another catalyst of architectural interest in the Palladian in the period before Wittkower's book was published.[12] We might surmise that it was not so much the publication of Wittkower's book that started the trend, nor the earlier publication of its central chapter, but rather the enormous impact of an article by his student Colin Rowe, who in 1947 had co-opted Wittkower's historical analysis for a sweeping comparison of the forms and principles of Palladianism with those of the modern movement, providing, by implication, a demand for "principles" in the creation of a truly modernist architecture for the present. This may explain why Smithson identified 1948, a year after the appearance of Rowe's article and a year before the appearance of Wittkower's book, as the year of Palladianism.

In November 1947, Colin Frederick Rowe submitted a 330-page thesis, "The Theoretical Drawings of Inigo Jones: Their Sources and Scope," to the Warburg Institute at the University of London "for the degree of M.A. in the History of Art," which was awarded in 1948. There was no preface or acknowledgments, but we know that in 1945 he was "Wittkower's only student," and that Fritz Saxl and Gertrude Bing were also involved. Saxl and Bing were, in Rowe's words, "highly impressed by it," and Wittkower himself, writing six years later, still thought it "a brilliant but unpublished" thesis.[13]

The structure of the thesis is simple enough. After a brief introduction to Inigo Jones, his biography, architectural formation, and "stylistic development," are three main parts: an essay on the "English architectural treatise" in relation to its Italian and English antecedents; a central section on what Rowe considers to be Jones's own treatise; and a third section that catalogs Jones's and John Webb's drawings "arranged," as Rowe puts it, "as a Treatise," that is, according to Rowe's own theory of how they might have been intended to be published.[14]

One will no doubt object that Jones neither wrote nor issued an architectural treatise beyond his posthumously published examination of Stonehenge as an antique Roman temple. But Rowe's thesis is that there exists a corpus of drawings, some by Jones himself, some by Webb, who worked in Jones's office, that represents the work in preparation for the publication of a major theoretical treatise on architecture, along the lines of those previously written and drawn by Serlio, Scamozzi, Palladio, and others, a treatise left incomplete and unpublished at Jones's death: "The content and schematic feeling of the drawings [of this group] recall irresistibly the characteristics of the Renaissance architectural treatise," Rowe writes, and "It is the object of this thesis to establish that these drawings represent the preliminary studies for such a theoretical work on architecture" (TDIJ, 2).

In other words, Rowe's own thesis consists of a theoretical argument for a theoretical treatise for which no written evidence exists, and the planned existence of which relies on visual identification alone. According to Rowe, the evidence of his visual inspection "suggests a preconceived system" comparable to those developed by earlier architects of the Renaissance. In this way, Rowe, who was never able to sustain the writing of a complete and fully developed treatise of his own, began his career as "a didactic exponent of architectural education" (as he characterized Jones) by completing (if not inventing) Inigo's own treatise for him. In the context of this symposium, Rowe's early thesis offers us much more evidence for his intellectual formation than the simple rearrangement of an archive, as he played Sherlock Holmes to Wittkower's Watson.

Completed in 1947, the same year as the publication of Rowe's "The Mathematics of the Ideal Villa," and three years before his "Mannerism and Modern Architecture," the thesis gives us a precise understanding of the development of his idea of Palladianism in its first iteration. Indeed, the true subject of the thesis might be seen to be Palladio rather than Jones or, more specifically, Jones as the eponymous hero of English Palladianism, heir to the mannerism of the late Renaissance and precursor of Burlington and Kent, and perhaps even the first neoclassicist.

This is not the place for an extended treatment of what emerges as an extraordinary synthesis of historical interpretation and formal analysis derived from Wölfflin and Wittkower, one that, so to speak, can be seen as constituting Rowe's mature approach. Nor can one do justice to the thesis as a whole, which, read today, remains one of the most succinct studies of the nature and role of the Renaissance treatise in Italy and England. In the present context, however, two aspects of the work stand out as informing our reading of the seminal articles, "Mathematics of the Ideal Villa" and "Mannerism and Modern Architecture." The first is Rowe's intellectual construction of Palladio—Jones's model and standard—as theoretician and systematizer of the Renaissance tradition: "In the school of Palladio the diverse elements [of Renaissance architecture] become classicised, and absorbed into an academic repertoire, which was to provide a European model" (TDIJ, 17). In his "architectural conservatism" and his neo-Platonic sympathies, Palladio "prolonged the Renaissance urge toward scientific clarity, reinforced his archeological preoccupations with a persuasive emotional depth, and a serious reserve of looseness and flexibility"(TDIJ, 17). More interested in ideal harmonies than antique remains, Palladio found in the printed treatise a perfect vehicle for his own project. According to Rowe, the *Quattro Libri dell'Architettura* was the most influential of all treatises, as "those accurate, and austerely programmatic pages" provided an "intelligible architecture, and the apparatus of artistic judgement for the Protestant world" (TDIJ, 18). Palladio's treatise, Rowe wrote,

> *is a methodical conception of the ancient world, which combines the dramatic qualities of Mannerism, with that voluntary sense of abstraction and balance, which Alberti had shown . . . Palladio always proceeds by way of the specific, to his generalisation; and it is in this quality of rational embodiment that his compelling power seems always to lie. The particular admirations of Mannerism are reduced to a scheme analogous to that order which the Renaissance had postulated* (TDIJ, 64–65).

Second, if Palladio was understood to be the synthesizer of Renaissance values and forms, Jones emerges in Rowe's account as the transmitter and historicizer of Palladio. Eclectic in the face of what Rowe characterizes as the "ambiguous inheritance" of Rome and Venice, Jones used his edition of the *Quattro Libri* as model, standard, and commonplace book, jotting his observations of Palladio's buildings as he visited them, writing notes on Palladio as well as recording observations on his own projects in the margins. For Jones, "The Palladian villa system offered a focus for the development of a whole complex of outside ideas." References to the antique and its mannerist reconstructions, to Scamozzi's classicism, to the restrained expansion of early baroque were all "regulated by a continual reference to Palladian ideals of scale and intelligibility" (TDIJ, 27). Rowe, through a careful formal analysis of Jones's designs from the Banqueting House on, demonstrates the emergence of an academicism that gradually appears in Jones's developed style of historicism, intellectualism, and academic correctness: "An eclectic with a natural restraint and classical bias, he evolved from a decorative and graceful early style, through a period of historicism, in which a Mannerist element is implicit, to a final period, where a classicism is imposed upon this Mannerist basis" (TDIJ, 45). We are thus presented with a thesis of Jones, systematizer of the systematizer, as he builds up a collection of more than two hundreds plates in readiness for their publication as the first English equivalent of Palladio's *Quattro Libri*.

This double inheritance, or transmission, of the Renaissance would be of simply academic interest if it did not form the basis of Rowe's own historical view of architecture in general and of the modern movement in particular. As elaborated in the London essays of 1947–50 and later reinforced by articles written during the Texas period of 1954–56, Rowe's modernism referred directly to the Palladianism of this first iteration in two fundamental respects: its crystallization in the work of a single "systematizer," in this case, Le Corbusier; and its propagation through a central written treatise, in this case, *Vers une architecture*. It relied on the initial experiments of two generations of multiple innovators, from the Arts and Crafts movement to expressionism, and on the completion of a few synthetic, paradigmatic works that encapsulated its ideals and their formal representation—the Villas Stein and Savoye. It also relied, apparently paradoxically for one who was ostensibly opposed to the very notion of progress in history, on a coherent theory of the historical zeitgeist for its assumptions of coherence and periodization. As Rowe noted in the comments he drafted in 1954 for the use of Harwell Harris, chairman of the Department of Architecture at Austin, "It cannot be assumed that the present day is without an overt artistic urge, will, volition. No earlier time has been without one and there is no reason to believe that we are exempted from what has so far been universal. That modern architecture is not merely a negative rationalism, that it embodies a positive will, is proved by evidences which are daily before our eyes."[15]

In this subsequent affirmation of Hegel, Riegl, Worringer, and Wölfflin, Rowe was simply making explicit the underlying premises of his master's thesis. That there was something called mannerism and mannerists was entirely assumed, even as such a movement was operating on established Renaissance codes and translating them into academic formulas for succeeding generations, thereby transforming the nature of mannerism itself. The process of identification and classification of the procedures and forms of modernism was more fluid, but its art historical method was equally well-established.

Convinced, like many of his generation—Banham and Colquhoun in Great Britain, Clement Greenberg and Leo Steinberg in the United States—that the first era of the modern avant-gardes was historically complete, Rowe saw his task with respect to the postwar practice of architecture and architectural history as defined on the one hand by the ideological and formal residue of avant-gardism and on the other by the much longer trajectory of architectural tradition since the Renaissance. In the process, as developed in his articles published between 1947 and 1960, he constructed a formulation of a more or less unified modernism that served as a critical armature for the rest of his life. Like Greenberg seeking to invent a similar modernism for painting, and countering the modern movement's own myth of the "end of history," Rowe turned to history as a key to the isolation of specifically modernist moves in architecture, as well as to more traditional survivals. His architectural analysis, out of Wölfflin and Wittkower, was, like Greenberg's approach to the canvas, neo-Kantian. If Greenberg sought to identify the roots and definition of modernism out of the emerging "flatness" of painting after Manet, Rowe turned back further, to the Renaissance (as Tafuri would later), as the touchstone of a developed architectural manner. The modernism thus defined by both Rowe and Greenberg from their quite different perspectives was, as Terry Eagleton has characterized that of T. S. Eliot, founded on a "Janus-faced temporality, in which one turns to the resources of the pre-modern in order to move backwards into a future that has transcended modernity altogether."[16]

In this context, Rowe's initial comparison of Palladio and Le Corbusier was neither the arbitrary result of a fashionable conceit adopted by a few young members of Team X and the Independent Group after a casual reading of Wittkower nor a Sunday conversation at Banham's house. Rather, for Rowe, Le Corbusier had, already by 1930, emerged as the Palladio of modernity. In 1959, Rowe wrote that Le Corbusier's influence, like Palladio's,

> has been principally exercised through the medium of the illustrated book; and if we wish to understand its nature, it is to his early treatise, Towards a New Architecture, and to the publication of his buildings and projects as his Oeuvre Complète that we must look. For in these books he evolves a frame of reference, persuades us to accept it, poses the problems, and answers them in his own terms; so that, like the great system makers of the Renaissance, Le Corbusier presents himself to us as a kind of living encyclopaedia of architecture, or as the index to a world where all experience is ordered and all inconsistency eradicated.[17]

This is not so much Palladio *and* Le Corbusier, mannerism *and* modern architecture, as it is "Le Corbusier = Palladian" and "modern architecture = mannerism." Of course, the "mannerists" themselves were not in any sense setting out with such a goal. To the contrary, for Rowe, they were the bold contrarians of their age. The supposedly blank panels of the Villa Schwob and the Casa di Palladio were construed respectively, and respectfully, within the codes of modernism and "the architectural traditions of Renaissance humanism."[18] What Rowe identified as Palladio's "inversion of the normal" and Le Corbusier's "formal ambiguity" were intended deliberately to "disrupt the inner core" of classical and modernist coherence. But equally, as Dvorak, Pevsner, and Wittkower had suggested, such disruption was far from classical in its historical implications; rather it was a sign of a "universal malaise" and of fundamental "inner contradictions" that afflicted classicism and modernism alike.

Here we find a clue to the later development of Rowe's increasing disenchantment with modernism. For given his historicist sense of a beginning, middle, and academic end to every stylistic movement, the parallel of the Renaissance systematized in Palladianism and Palladianism slipping into late-eighteenth-century neoclassicism with that of an increasingly ossified modernism was too strong to resist. As Rowe concluded his review of the 1959 exhibition of Le Corbusier at the Building Centre, "The success of any revolution is also its failure." Modern architecture was now ubiquitous, an "official art." Rather than "the continuing symbol of something new, Modern architecture has recently become the decoration of everything existing."[19] Even as the neo-Palladian villa "at its best, became the picturesque object in the English park," so Le Corbusier—"source of innumerable pastiches and of tediously amusing exhibition techniques"—is rendered empty as "le style Corbu." As Rowe had concluded in "Mathematics of the Ideal Villa," "It is the magnificently realisable quality of the originals which one fails to find in the works of neo-Palladians and exponents of 'le style Corbu.' The difference is that between the universal and the decorative or merely competent; perhaps in both cases it is the adherence to rules which has lapsed."[20]

Thus, already in 1947, we may identify that sense of exhaustion, of the already seen, of the endlessly repeated formulas that pervades his assessments of contemporary work, as if the critic/historian is, Spengler-like, already wasted by the ennui of living at the end of history. In this wasteland only Stirling seems to have surmounted the transition from mannerism to neoclassicism, as a latter-day John Soane, eclectic and combinatory, abstract and symbolic, parading whatever *virtù* might be salvaged from a formalism without ideology, a rhetoric without content from the very force of its jangled inversions. In the face of such bravado, it would seem that, for the connoisseur of decadence at least, the tightly controlled languages of the Five and the rationally revived typologies of the neorationalists were little more than entertaining decorations of an already worn-out repertoire. This would, of course, emerge as a long and difficult process of resignation and blocked utopianism in Rowe's own writing and teaching. But that, as they say, is another story.

1. Christopher Wren, *Parentalia* (1750), as cited in Colin Rowe, "The Mathematics of the Ideal Villa: Palladio and Le Corbusier Compared," *Architectural Review,* March 1947, 101.

2. Charles Jencks, *Modern Movements in Architecture* (1973), cited on the dust jacket of Colin Rowe, *The Mathematics of the Ideal Villa and Other Essays* (Cambridge, Mass.: MIT Press, 1976); Reyner Banham, "Actual Monuments," in *A Critic Writes: Essays by Reyner Banham,* ed. Mary Banham et al. (Berkeley and Los Angeles: University of California Press, 1996), 282.

3. Alexander Caragonne, cited on the dust jacket of Colin Rowe, *As I Was Saying: Recollections and Miscellaneous Essays,* ed. Alexander Caragonne, 3 vols. (Cambridge, Mass.: MIT Press, 1996).

4. Colin Rowe, introduction to *Five Architects: Eisenman, Graves, Gwathmey, Hejduk, Meier* (New York: Oxford University Press, 1972, 1975), 7.

5. Rowe, erratum slip, *Five Architects.*

6. Rowe, "Program versus Paradigm: Otherwise Casual Notes on the Pragmatic, the Typical and the Possible" (1980–83), *As I Was Saying,* vol. 2, 27–28.

7. Reyner Banham, "The New Brutalism," *Architectural Review,* December 1955, 361.

8. For an extended discussion of the New Palladianism in Britain in the 1940s, see Henry Millon, "Rudolf Wittkower, *Architectural Principles in the Age of Humanism:* Its Influence on the Development and Interpretation of Modern Architecture," *Journal of the Society of Architectural Historians* 31 (1972): 83–91.

9. "Report of a Debate on the Notion 'that Systems of Proportion Make Good Design Easier and Bad Design More Difficult,'" *RIBA Journal* 64 (1957): 461.

10. A. G. Butler, review of *Architectural Principles in the Age of Humanism,* by Rudolf Wittkower, *RIBA Journal* 59 (1951): 59–60.

11. Alison and Peter Smithson, letter to the editor, *RIBA Journal* 59 (1952): 140–41.

12. Wittkower published his three essays on Renaissance architecture, which made up the bulk of *Architectural Principles,* in the *Journal of the Warburg and Courtauld Institutes* between 1940 and 1945: "Alberti's Approach to Antiquity in Architecture," *Journal of the Warburg and Courtauld Institutes* 4 (1940–41): 1–18; "Principles of Palladio's Architecture," pt. 1, *Journal of the Warburg and Courtauld Institutes* 7 (1944): 102–22; and "Principles of Palladio's Architecture," pt. 2, *Journal of the Warburg and Courtauld Institutes* 8 (1945): 68–106. The last essay included the celebrated plate "Schematized Plans of Eleven of Palladio's Villas," which was used so effectively by Rowe in his comparison of Palladio and Le Corbusier.

13. Rudolf Wittkower, "Inigo Jones, Architect and Man of Letters," *RIBA Journal* 60 (1953). Reprinted in Wittkower, *Palladio and English Palladianism* (London: Thames and Hudson, 1974), 51–66: "We know that there exist about 200 theoretical drawings coming from Inigo's office and mainly drawn by John Webb, probably during the 1640s. For a good many years I believed that the puzzle of these drawings becomes intelligible if one assumes that they were made in preparation for an architectural treatise. Now a pupil of mine, Colin Rowe, has substantiated this

assumption in a brilliant but unpublished thesis to which Dr. Whinney has already referred in the *RIBA Journal,* June 1952. As was customary in Italy, the first book of Inigo's treatise would have dealt with the system of the orders. A fair number of meticulously executed drawings of the orders by the hand of John Webb are extant and among them is the Ionic order which is very similar to the order Inigo has used about twenty years before in the Banqueting House."

14. Colin Rowe, "The Theoretical Drawings of Inigo Jones: Their Sources and Scope" (unpublished thesis, University of London, November 1947) (hereafter cited in the text as TDIJ).

15. Rowe, *As I Was Saying,* vol. 1, 47.

16. Eliot was, of course, a central reference for both Rowe and Greenberg; for the former, he represented a position dedicated to the essential roots of talent in tradition ("Ideas, Talents, Poetics: A Problem of Manifesto," 1987) and a champion of the "virtues and the values of the ambiguous and the difficult" ("Ideas, Talents," postscript, 1994); for the latter, an opponent worthy of his most lucid and extended essay from the 1950s, "The Plight of Our Culture," yet an opponent whose "definition of culture," however elitist and conservative, tested to its limits Greenberg's own definition of modern cultural production in its opposition to "kitsch."

17. Colin Rowe, "Le Corbusier: Utopian Architect," *As I Was Saying,* vol. 1, 137. This article was first published in the *Listener* on February 12, 1959.

18. Colin Rowe, "Mannerism and Modern Architecture," *Mathematics of the Ideal Villa,* 33.

19. Rowe, *As I Was Saying,* vol. 1, 136.

20. Rowe, "Mathematics of the Ideal Villa," 104.

URBANISM

Figures, Fields, Fragments

Stan Allen

Our panel has been charged with a double task. First, to contrast the ideas of urbanism in the work of Peter Eisenman and Leon Krier; and second, to position their 1977 debate in the context of the precedents of Piranesi and Nolli. The assumption here is that the work of the two eighteenth-century delineators can shed some light on contrasting ways of thinking about architecture and the city in the present.

History, of course, did not stop in 1977. Any discussion of urbanism must also take into account the real changes in the city itself over the past twenty-five years and the way in which the practices of urbanism have evolved. What in the late 1970s could convincingly be framed as a debate between traditional urbanism and avant-garde experimentalism must today account for a third position—a whole series of loosely allied practices that are identified with the complex realities of the late-twentieth-century global metropolis. Not the urbanism of Rome (or Atlantis) but the urbanisms of Las Vegas, Tokyo, New York, Shanghai, São Paulo, Atlanta, or Houston. These would necessarily include the procedures and protocols of popular culture, digital technologies, urban infrastructure, datascaping, scenario planning, edge cities, shopping malls, minority subcultures, and nomad populations: urbanisms that emphasize process and program over form and place. Rem Koolhaas and OMA are clearly an important point of reference here, but they are only one among many, including, for example, the emergence of landscape urbanism, with its attention to ecology and adaptation. If the only alternative to traditional urbanism were avant-garde experimentalism, Krier would win hands down. Fortunately, the world is a bigger place than that, and there are viable alternatives emerging all the time. While I admire the historical conceit of taking a cross section of the architectural debates of the 1970s, and while I recognize the explanatory value of the Nolli/Piranesi opposition within that cross section, any discussion of urbanism today is radically incomplete without a recognition of these more recent practices.

James Corner Field Operations/Stan Allen Architect, Fresh Kill Reserve, competition, 2001.

Like many others here, I hold some stake in this recent history. I readily agreed to participate in this conference because this was a debate that marked my own years as an architecture student, and I had my moments of sympathy with both sides. Naively, I also agreed because I thought it would be easy. I spent a lot of time looking at and writing about Piranesi in the mid-1980s.[1] But just as the original debate between Eisenman and Krier was marked by issues of the late 1970s—typology, morphology, and questions of history, memory, and the role of the avant-garde—the work I did in the mid-1980s was marked by architecture's fascination with formal and conceptual strategies based on disjunction: fragmentation, montage and collage, and associated conceptual frameworks of deconstruction and institutional critique. At that time, I was interested in the possibility of rereading Piranesi's plan notations and of finding productive new architectural strategies by returning to a moment when the classical and the modernist impulses were held in an uncomfortable proximity. I don't claim that this was a new strategy. Manfredo Tafuri's writings on Piranesi enabled later generations to see past the sometimes picturesque character of Piranesi's engravings to the deep, unresolved architectural contradictions that inform all of his work. For Tafuri, these contradictions are symptomatic of still unresolved tensions that underlie modernity itself. I was aware of Eisenman's artificial "excavations," which were influenced by Tafuri's readings of Piranesi, and the writings of Jennifer Bloomer and others, who, under the influence of deconstruction, pushed Tafuri's arguments to a more delirious endpoint. There is also a tectonic trajectory emerging from Piranesi that has its origins in the 1960s, when Louis Kahn turned to the *Campo Marzio* drawings as a model for an elemental architecture that carried forward the dignity of Roman construction without the decorative character of its Beaux-Arts translations. The work I did at that time was also marked by my experience working in Spain on Rafael Moneo's Museum of Roman Art at Mérida, itself a sophisticated reworking of Piranesian space and tectonics. All that is interesting as background, but none of it really seems useful to address the overriding question of urbanism in the work of Eisenman and Krier.

Therefore, I would like to defer the Nolli/Piranesi question for a moment and speak instead to the issue of urbanism. And this is where I have some difficulty, because, as I see it, there is no urbanism in Eisenman. This should not really be controversial. I do not mean to suggest, as some New Urbanist critics have, that Eisenman's ideas are dangerous or destructive; his is simply a different research project. A coherent theory of urbanism was never a high priority in his work; there is an important difference between an architect working at the scale of the city and the practices of urbanism. At a certain moment in his career, Eisenman became fascinated with the city. But the city was interesting mainly as source material for the issues that had always fascinated him—that is to say, questions of memory, history, presence and absence, alienation, and language. Eisenman is principally concerned with the configuration of objects, not with the complex social fabric of the city. His architecture has always functioned as a self-referential index of the procedures of its own making. He is interested in the way in which history is inscribed in the city as memory traces, but he is not particularly interested in history or the city per se. In this work at least, Eisenman is fascinated by discontinuity, dislocation, and fragmentation, and he finds in the city a perfect example of a man-made construction marked by violent change. Eisenman's architecture performs a work of critical, hermeneutic intensification, making evident the gaps, seams, and dissonances that already exist in the text of the city. He quite purposefully resists architecture's *projective instrumentality*, that is to say, its ability to intervene and participate in the complex, interrelated flows of everyday life in the city or, perhaps, to heal some of those scars. Eisenman's idea of the architect as author simply does not allow for the collective and often anonymous production of urban space. He is instead a maker of monumental objects, which stand out from the fabric of the city and serve to remind the viewer of everything that is lost or broken in the city today. Hence, Eisenman's preferred subject is a reader of the city text, not an inhabitant or a citizen. All of this may be changing in Eisenman's contemporary practice, but in the Cannaregio project, in the artificial

Peter Eisenman, Biocentrum, J. W. Goethe University, Frankfurt am Main, 1987: model.

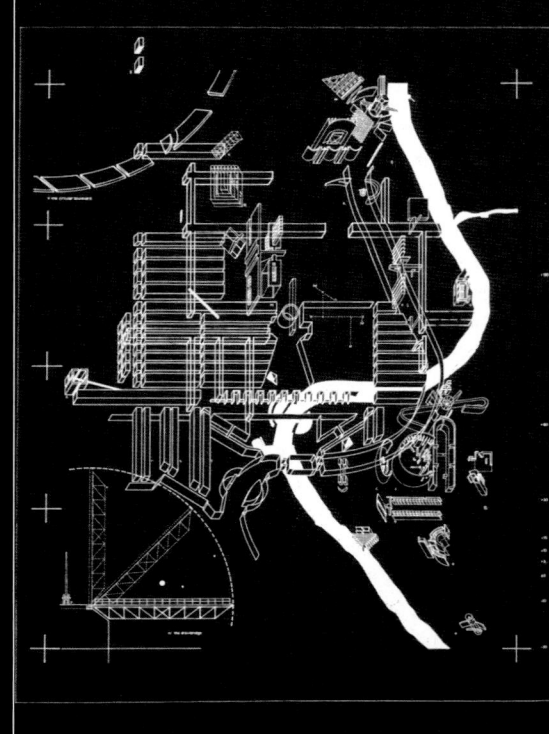

Stan Allen, *Reworking Piranesi,* 1986.

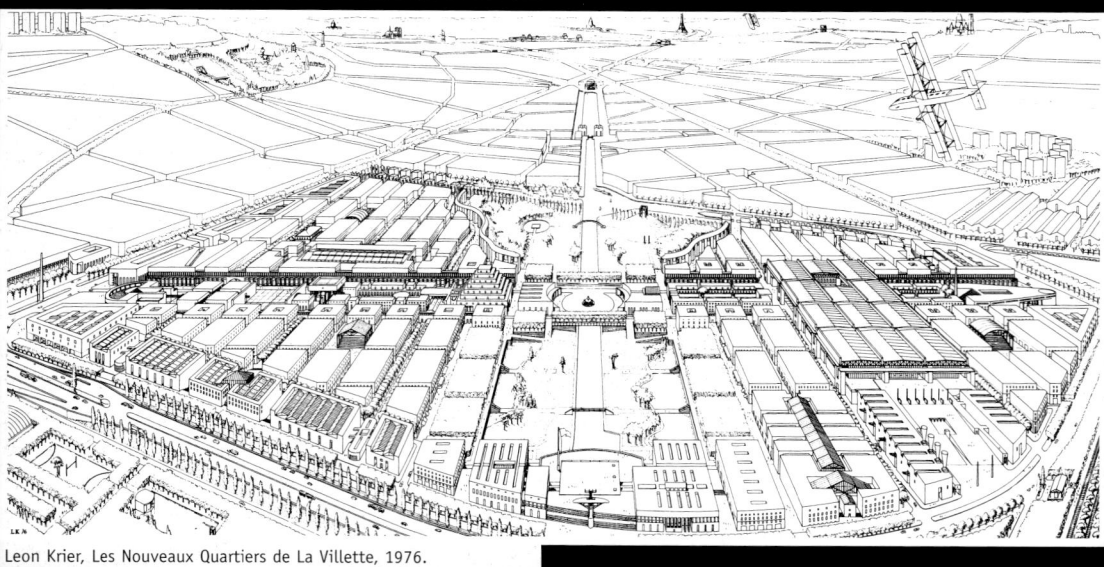

Leon Krier, Les Nouveaux Quartiers de La Villette, 1976.

excavations and Romeo and Juliet projects of the late 1970s and early 1980s, architecture is presented as a self-referential, interpretive machine, encompassing texts, drawings, models, and books, and requiring an effort of decoding to unravel the internal structure.

Krier, on the other hand, seems to promise everything that Eisenman lacks: a coherent urbanistic idea, a theory about the relationship between architecture and the city, and a practice that embraces architecture's ameliorative agency. Where Eisenman teases out discontinuity and memorializes loss, Krier wants to intervene as a planner and an architect to repair the wounds and make the body of the city whole again. He does so with the traditional tools of urbanism: street grids, typologies, axial boulevards, and monumental civic buildings. But the problem here is that the city—contemporary or traditional—has never been as unified or coherent as he imagines. As the artistic avant-gardes of the twentieth century understood, the city is the privileged place of difference and otherness. Our experience of the city is fundamentally fragmented and discontinuous. Anyone who reads Charles Dickens's accounts of nineteenth-century London or the historical records of life in the preindustrial cities that Krier so admires will have difficulty recognizing the picture of harmony that Krier draws. This is not to say that the city is inherently discontinuous, alienating, or fragmented, but that what is interesting about the city is that it is a place where meaningful difference and local discontinuity can exist within a framework of overall coherence. Cities are legible, orderly mechanisms that continue to serve the inhabitants who live and work there while also sponsoring cultures of contestation, alternative lifestyles, and minority populations. In other words, I am not so sure there is a viable *contemporary* urbanism in Krier, either.

In this context, it is useful to recall Anne Querrien's distinction between metropolis and capital, published, significantly enough, in the first issue of *Zone* (1986), a moment that represents the first opening of the discourse of contemporary urbanism away from the impasse of the Eisenman/Krier debate and out to other disciplines.[2] According to Querrien, the favored geometry of the capital is concentric, with power and control radiating from a fixed center. The metropolis, which originates in trade and communication, rather than national identity, favors the grid, both for its efficiency in organizing and managing territory and for its democratic equality. The capital wants to subjugate economic flux, while the metropolis tends to remove impediments to its free flow. "In short," Querrien writes, "the metropolis is not a center, and it has no center: made up of networks, it is itself caught up in a network of cities through which the flux of world economy circulates." The metropolis is cosmopolitan; it depends on economic exchange between strangers. It functions as a "membrane which allows communication between two or more milieus," whereas the capital "serves as a nucleus around which these milieus are rigorously organized." (Think of the difference between Washington, D.C., and New York, or of Rome as the paradigm of the imperial capital; modernist visions such as Brasilia or Chandigarh extend but do not significantly modify the model: they still maintain the geometric segregation of earlier forms.) While the capital tends to subsume minority populations under a single identity, the metropolis makes a place for minorities within its confines: "The metropolis puts an incongruous mix of beings into circulation . . . it is a place of experimentation, where new operational propositions can be made concerning current practices." Finally, the distinction between metropolis and capital is synchronic and reversible—one is not a stage on the way to the other, nor is one necessarily more advanced than the other. Elements of the capital persist in every metropolis and vice versa.

This tells us that it is not so much Krier's antipathy toward modern technology that prevents him from engaging with a fuller notion of contemporary urban life as it is something more ideological in his view of city culture itself. Krier lacks a theory of urbanism sufficiently robust and complex to account for the uncertainties of the contemporary metropolis precisely because he wants to regulate its promiscuous variety. Instead, he holds up something very like the capital as an urban ideal, while Eisenman, like his early-twentieth-century avant-garde

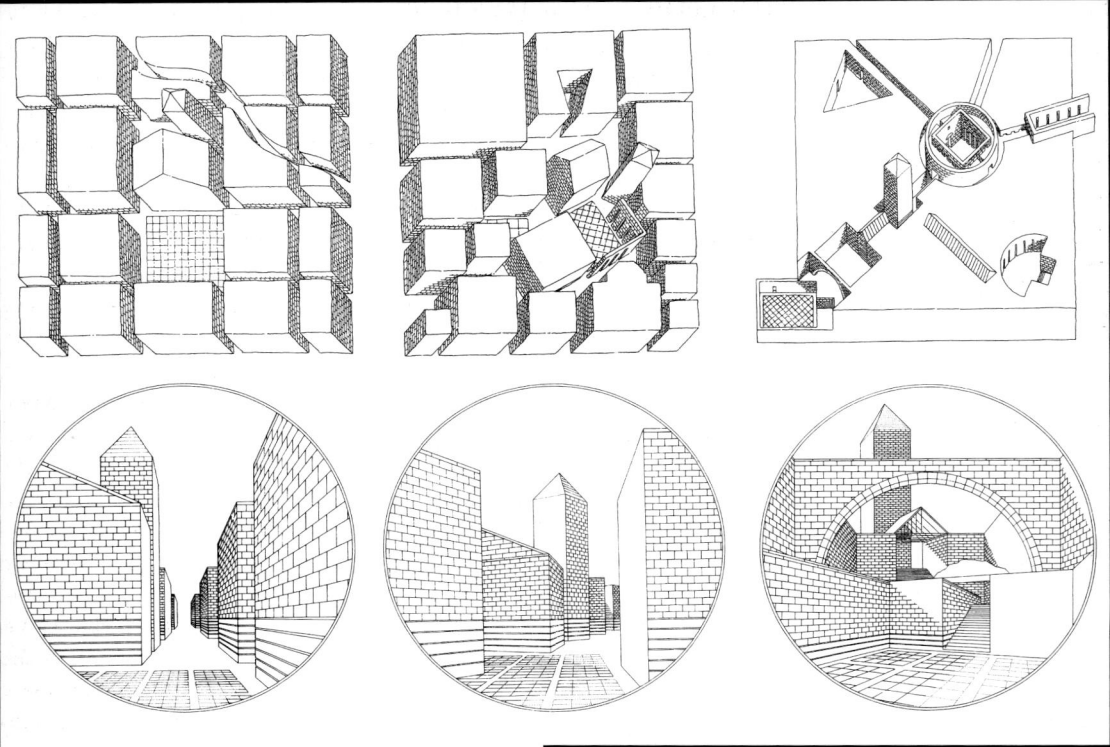

Leon Krier, *Three Categories of Urban Space,* 1977.

predecessors, finds in the metropolis a place of fragmentation and alienation that mirrors his own architectural preferences. While this distinction is clear, it deserves to be pointed out that Krier misses the discontinuity that inheres even in the capital, while Eisenman cannot see the urbanistic coherence of the metropolis—the essentially stable, overall fabric that is the necessary framework to local difference. Krier, in this respect, could be seen as a *diagrammatic* classicist—reproducing the patterns and forms of the traditional city without regard for the realities of everyday life. This suggests that classicism today, which claims authenticity above all, will always be thin and provisional, inevitably compromised with the scenographic. In this sense, Krier and Eisenman are not so far apart, each working with a formal language at odds with the reality of the contemporary city.

Contemporary urbanism needs procedures and concepts capable of holding together coherence and discontinuity in productive new mixtures. It needs to engage the real complexity of the city today, as the technologies, social life, and economic engines of urbanism continue to change. It needs to recognize the very real environmental crises of our time and the complexities of the natural and social ecologies at work in the city. Form making has a powerful agency and needs to be part of the toolbox, but form making alone cannot account for the complexity of the city. For this reason, neither Eisenman nor Krier (at least within this limited time span) seems to offer a way out.

Can the Nolli/Piranesi opposition help us out of this impasse? My sense is that, in fact, the Nolli/Piranesi pairing reinforces my argument. There is an implicit assumption in the alignment Eisenman/Piranesi versus

Krier/Nolli that suggests that, in urbanistic terms, Eisenman stands for fragmentation, dissolution, and alienation, while Krier stands for order and consistency. Eisenman is identified with the decentered subject of modernity; Krier, with the imagined unity of the subject in premodern times. However, this opposition is not as absolute as it appears. Eisenman, through Colin Rowe, is certainly indebted to Nolli, while Krier's plan strategies, filtered through James Stirling and Kahn, owe something to Piranesi. And I would argue that both Nolli and Piranesi structure the relationship between coherence and difference in complex ways not fully taken up by either Krier or Eisenman.

In contemporary architectural discourse, the reference to classical architecture is used as a shorthand for unity, order, and consistency. Eisenman and Krier are in complete agreement that classical architecture represents harmony, order, and stability, but they assign different values to that stability. The one sees fragmentation as pathology, while the other cultivates it as the architectural analogue of contemporary alienation. Eisenman needs stability to push against; Krier, to patch up what is broken. In this, they are fully consistent with the received traditions of architectural history. Heinrich Wölfflin, for example, writes in the late nineteenth century about the Renaissance centralized church using language like this: "Every line, inside and outside, seems to be conditioned by one central regularizing and unifying force . . . A state of fulfillment, of perfect being reigns throughout."[3]

Robin Evans, who was a great puncturer of the balloons of received opinion, questions this simple association of classical architecture with order and harmony, and I think his skepticism is justified. In "Perturbed Circles," the first chapter of his book *The Projective Cast*, Evans reexamines classical architecture's perceived stability. By asking an apparently obvious question such as "Where is the center of a centralized church?"[4] a founding assumption of so much architectural theorizing is itself thrown off center. Evans's game is not to expose a fault line at the base of classicism (laying bare one of classicism's founding myths) but to demonstrate the actual complexity of a supposedly fixed system. In the case of Evans's deceptively innocent question, the answer, not surprisingly, turns out to be that even the most conventional centralized churches have many centers. (He counts eight in Bramante's San Pietro in Montorio, for example.)[5] Evans makes a compelling argument for careful seeing and for giving visual evidence priority over theoretical generalization. If we look carefully at a complex and fully realized work of architecture, he suggests, we uncover a level of indeterminacy all the more provocative for its presence within a supposedly stable frame. This is not architecture's shortcoming but its source of continued power and interest—that is to say, its capacity to produce complex objects that will stand up to sustained examination without exhausting themselves in the obvious explanations.

Now this is not news that either Eisenman or Krier particularly wants to hear. Both flatten classicism for their own purposes. Krier makes diagrams of classical monuments that will stand out from the ordinary fabric of the city, while Eisenman understands the classical as the stable ground against which deformation is registered. Both subscribe to the fiction that "human consciousness suddenly fell out of a world with an edge and a center, as in an uncomfortable awakening,"[6] and they deploy similar strategies of figure and field to different ends. These distinct views of architecture as a practice in turn inform their use of sources, including Nolli and Piranesi.

Applying Evans's criteria of close attention to the visual evidence, it is possible to outline some important differences between these eighteenth-century architects. Nolli and Piranesi were contemporaries, and Piranesi even contributed engravings to Nolli's large map of Rome. Nolli, trained as a surveyor, was only recognized as an architect after the completion and publication of his maps. Piranesi was an architect who built little, but his vision was insistently three-dimensional. And while Nolli set out to record the Rome that stood in his own time, Piranesi engaged in a complex historical fiction of the city. Working from the fragments of the Roman past embedded in the city of the present, his reconstruction is inevitably speculative. Hence Nolli's

Leonardo da Vinci, architectural drawings from MS "B," c. 1489 or later.

map provides a comprehensive, measurable overview aligned with the instrumentality of organized city planning, while Piranesi's maps are fragmentary and unreliable in their anticipation of the critical narratives of the twentieth-century avant-gardes.

Nolli's map registers the traditional devices of baroque planning—axes, arcades, and monuments—against the continuous weave of public space that is the map's most remarked-upon feature. As a graphic instrument, it reduces the city to only a few variables—white for streets and public spaces, black for monuments, and a hatched gray for the anonymous fabric of the city—and in so doing establishes continuity where no continuity exists. On the other hand, inasmuch as the Nolli map records the texture of a city that has grown organically over time, it records all of the imperfections, irregularities, and inconsistencies that are the natural outcome of the life of the city in time. Krier attempts to replicate this texture, with its clear distinction between public and private, its registration of architectural difference, and its background of continuous urban fabric. His methodology is to contrast monuments (civic space) with fabric—space for work and living. The grid is the preferred organizing device for the fabric (a compromise with pragmatic modern city planning); for monuments, he uses a figural vocabulary that owes something to Piranesi, among others. All of the fine-grained texture and real difference of a city that has grown over time is compressed. Krier's version is a snapshot of a process that in the actual city unfolds over a long, discontinuous time line.

As Gregory Bateson (among others) has pointed out, the map is not the territory. Every map works by exclusion, and every map is subjective. What gets onto the map, according to Bateson, are differences, and someone has to decide which differences make a difference. In the case of Nolli, the city has been encoded according to two interlocking binary distinctions: built fabric/public space and ordinary fabric/monument. The map is a powerful tool, but many differences have been left out—block structure, height, typology, land ownership, infrastructure, program, and so forth; in other words, most of the variables of contemporary urbanism. To the extent that Krier, like Rowe, privileges the Nolli figure/ground, all of the flows—of money, matter, and energy—that drive the building of cities today are absent.

In the American context, Nolli is associated not so much with Krier as with Rowe and the *Roma Interrotta* exhibition and publication of 1978–79. This project, although organized and curated by others, emerged out of Rowe and Fred Koetter's book *Collage City* and their notion of a compositional unity that allowed competing fragments in the city to coexist within a larger framework, just as the checks and balances of constitutional democracy allow for individual expression within a larger, unified whole. The fragmentary, "interrupted" quality of Nolli's plan is emphasized, and the fabric is understood as a medium in which moments of compositional intensity are suspended and insulated from one another. But the coherence is by and large an effect of Nolli's graphic equality rather than the imagined experience of the city. In his introduction to the published version of *Roma Interrotta*, Michael Graves contrasts the "mutually adjusted set pieces" of Piranesi's *Campo Marzio* to the "comprehensible equity between figural object and figural space" in Nolli's map of Rome. He recognizes that this sets up a problem having to do with the fragmentary character of the plan: "What begins as a problematic condition of mutual adjustments between the fragmented sections of the Nolli plan as issued to each of the 12 architects can be used positively by assuming that the city is one of mutually adjusted fragments, or adjacencies, modified to fit the context, rather than set pieces in the field." In other words, a working vocabulary of fragments is a given, which is compensated for by adjustments to and within the context. This is another simulation of the real give and take of city growth over time, dependent on the fragment/field opposition. Discontinuity is not rejected; rather, it is tempered by its absorption within a resilient and graphically continuous fabric.

Both Piranesi and Nolli, then, entered contemporary architecture under the sign of the fragment. In Nolli, that fragmentation was tempered by a continuous adjustment of figure/ground protocols; in Piranesi, such mediation is absent, and the results are clearly more radical. For Tafuri, the *Campo Marzio* is a "formless heap of fragments" and a "colossal piece of *bricolage*." The "obsessive reiteration of the inventions," he writes, "reduces the whole organism to a sort of gigantic, 'useless machine.'"[7] Joseph Rykwert refers to Piranesi's "necrophiliac passion for the glory of ancient Rome," and Sergei Eisenstein, to a "madness" in the "juxtapositions which explode the very foundation of the objects' customary possibility." Where the Nolli plan compresses the passage of time, Piranesi exaggerates the effects of decay and deterioration.

The Campo Marzio is itself displaced from the historical center of Rome, and the city that Piranesi depicts is a very strange animal. Lying outside the city walls, the Campo Marzio had traditionally been the site of funerals and burials, and indeed, the plan is dominated by two immense funerary monuments (to Augustus and Hadrian). Buildings devoted to military use, the culture of the body, and spectacle dominate, as would be expected on a site dedicated to the god of war: there are armories, stadiums, gymnasiums, amphitheaters and circuses, gardens and pleasure fountains, crypts and tombs. On the other hand, there are no civic institutions, streets are nonexistent, and there is no domestic fabric in this city. The map is an elaborate historical fiction. Actual Roman monuments from the Severan Marble Plan, for example, can be located in the *Campo Marzio,* but not in their proper locations. It is no surprise that, after Freud, after surrealism, and after deconstruction, Piranesi emerges as a privileged point of reference.

For Tafuri, Piranesi's project is a futile attempt to absorb the contradictions of an architectural language on the brink of falling apart, a kind of "shock treatment" applied to architecture's foundations in the effort to postpone inevitable collapse. He describes a battle of architecture against itself. The city's ability to absorb these highly charged fragments and to provide some mediating framework is stressed to the limit; the city itself is shown to be comprised entirely of fragmented objects. In Piranesi's vision of the city, there is no preexisting unity that has been fragmented; rather, the broken and discontinuous fragments now constitute the starting point, the "degraded means" with which, as Piranesi puts it, architecture is now "condemned" to operate. Like a detective or an analyst, the architect's job is now to find some way to make sense out of this "heap of fragments."

And yet, for all of Tafuri's apocalyptic statements (which seemed to resonate so well with the architectural climate of the 1980s), architecture has not collapsed. The architecture in Piranesi is legible and systematic, and it can be productively reread in different contexts. All the rules of symmetry, axiality, and hierarchy are in place. The limits of architecture as language have been tested in Piranesi, but architecture persists. You could say that architecture survives the loss of the city; compositional figures retain their individual autonomy—they touch but do not compromise one another. I would suggest that there is a fairly exact parallel here with Eisenman. Eisenman, too, wants to test the limits of architecture, but he still wants his deformations to remain legible. He needs some norm to work against. He is invested in the "architecturalness" of his project, that is to say, in the maintenance of architecture as a more or less coherent system, with rules that are collectively understood, so that his own radical agency can be registered against a stable framework. His project is still an ontological one, which asks, what is architecture and where are its limits?

Eisenman is further wedded to a notion of history as some sort of discontinuous continuum in which individual gaps and seams appear but the fabric as a whole remains intact. In Eisenman, as in Piranesi, the representational structure accommodates a newly discovered formal dynamism in order to preserve its own intrinsic structure. Tafuri's characterization of the way in which an earlier avant-garde reread Piranesi could well apply to Eisenman: "Deprived of its utopian potential and of its ideology . . . [the avant-garde] can only fall back upon itself; it can only explore the stages of its own development. At best, it may recognize the ambiguity of its own origins."[8]

IL CAMPO MARZIO DELL'ANTICA ROMA

OPERA DI G. B. PIRANESI
SOCIO DELLA REAL SOCIETÀ
DEGLI ANTIQUARI DI LONDRA

Giovanni Battista Piranesi, Il Campo Marzio (detail), 1762.

Postscript

Merely to think about cities and get somewhere, one of the main things to know is what kind of a problem cities pose, for all problems cannot be thought about in the same way.

—Jane Jacobs, *The Death and Life of Great American Cities*

I started off by asserting that I did not find a convincing urbanism in either Krier or Eisenman—I am aware that this statement is open to challenge. It requires a definition of urbanism, and in order to do that, you have to ask what sort of problem the city poses as an object of study. To suggest today that the city is a problem of organized complexity is almost self-evident. Complexity is a buzzword today, but it is important to be more precise. The organized complexity of the city is a bottom-up, qualitative complexity—where a relatively small number of interacting variables create complex effects—rather than a quantitative complexity of accretion, distortion, or deformation (as in Piranesi, for example). Steven Johnson, in his recent book *Emergence: The Connected Lives of Ants, Brains, Cities and Software*, traces this notion from more recent sources, such as the mathematical models proposed by economist Paul Krugman in his 1995 lectures "The Self Organizing Economy" and back to Jane Jacobs and her descriptions of the city in *The Death and Life of Great American Cities*, written in the early 1960s. As Johnson shows, Jacobs's populism and love of the intimate, local scale are based on a sophisticated understanding of the city as a complex, interactive field condition: "Under the seeming disorder of the old city," she writes, "is a marvelous order for maintaining the safety of the streets and the freedom of the city. It is a complex order ... composed of movement and change ... The ballet of the good city sidewalk never repeats itself from place to place, and in one place is always replete with new improvisations."

When Jacobs writes, as she does elsewhere, that "the city happens to be a problem in organized complexity," she is referring to distinctions elaborated by Warren Weaver in 1958. Weaver outlines three stages in the development of scientific thinking. In the first stage (from the seventeenth to the nineteenth centuries), the physical sciences developed analytical techniques for handling problems with a limited number of variables—the classical problems of motion, pressure, and temperature. "Simplicity," Weaver notes, "was a condition for progress at that stage of development of science." In the early part of the twentieth century, techniques were developed to deal with problems characterized by a large number of variables—questions of probability and statistical mechanics that may not be predictable in individual instances but that as a system possess orderly, average properties or patterns. This he calls "disorganized complexity." It was not until well into the twentieth century that a third class of problem began to be addressed seriously. These are problems with a relatively small number of variables—small, compared to the number of atoms in, say, a cylinder of gas, but larger than the two or three variables of classical physics. Moreover, in the life sciences, where these problems tend to appear, the variables are all organically interrelated. "These problems," he notes, "as contrasted with the disorganized situations with which statistics can cope, *show the essential feature of organization*. We shall therefore refer to this group of problems as those of *organized complexity* ... They are all problems which involve a *sizable number of factors which are interrelated into an organic whole*." These insights have, of course, been subsequently much more fully developed in a variety of scientific disciplines, but Weaver's remains a concise definition. Architecture's response so far has been primarily metaphorical.

The fit in our case is quite close. Krier wants to turn back the clock to a time when the city could be reduced to a few easily predictable variables, and he ends up with a diagram of the traditional city. Eisenman loves the uncertainty and indeterminacy of disorganized complexity, which he elaborates as a formal engine to produce undecidable architectural configurations. Both Eisenman and Krier perhaps need to ignore some of the complexity of the city in order to productively harness its formal

Andreas Gursky, *Tokyo Stock Exchange,* 1990.

energy in their own architectural production. But in my view, we have to pay close attention to the difficult and always variable order of the city itself. Productive work in the future will build upon—or radicalize—these insights from an earlier period and understand the city as a problem in organized complexity—that is to say, a dynamic system in which a relatively small number of variables interact in complex formations to create unexpected and only partially controllable wholes: gradient fields in which figure and difference emerge from within the field rather than being delineated as fragments, whether modern or classical, against an artificially stabilized ground.

1. See Stan Allen, "Piranesi's *Campo Marzio:* An Experimental Design," *Assemblage* 10 (1989).

2. Anne Querrien, "The Metropolis and the Capital," *Zone* 1–2 (1986): 219–21.

3. Cited in Robin Evans, *The Projective Cast: Architecture and Its Three Geometries* (Cambridge, Mass.: MIT Press, 1995), 3.

4. Evans, *Projective Cast,* 6.

5. Evans, *Projective Cast,* 9.

6. Evans, *Projective Cast,* 103.

7. Manfredo Tafuri, *Architecture and Utopia: Design and Capitalist Development* (1973; English trans., Cambridge, Mass.: MIT Press, 1987), 15.

8. Manfredo Tafuri, "The Dialectic of the Avant-Garde," *Oppositions* 11:79.

A Funny Thing Happened on the Way to the Forum: The Nolli Plan and Other Italian Jobs

R. E. Somol

> To get out, go deeper.
> —Roland Barthes

Powers of 10
A couple of paperhangers—that's what we would have called them in the old days. In 1977, it was still possible to make a name and a couple of quick bucks by passing off funny paper and counterfeit cities in the better galleries around town, a venerable tradition of grift that went back to the heyday of mid-eighteenth-century printmakers. Of course, Rome has been the currency of choice for such swindles for generations of architect-forgers returning there for one last shot at the big score, or in an attempt to erase evidence from the scene of a crime already committed. But it's all ancient history today: twenty-five years ago, it was Peter Eisenman and Leon Krier; two hundred fifty, it was Nolli and Piranesi. Paradoxically, maybe we have to go back 2,500 years on this retrospective tour, to Romulus and Remus, to see if there are any contemporary lessons for pulling off the successful caper today.

How, then, is 1977 different from now? What are the funny things—the unpredictable events, the mistranslations—that occurred on the way back to the Forum, to Rome, that turned all of those plans on end? While it may only be hearsay, Donald Barthelme said, "The death of God left the angels in a strange position." By the same token, the death of modernism left urbanism in an equally tough spot. As Stan Allen suggested, there is some real doubt over the extent to which urbanism exists in the work of Eisenman and Krier. In large part, this suspicion results from the consistent critique that both have leveled against modernism, which at a minimum implies serious reservations about the possible performances of urbanism.

The Two Caesars of Criticality
Despite the distraction of their quarter-century of shadowboxing (or is it simply a case of assuming roles for the ultimate success of the sting?), Krier and Eisen-

Giovanni Battista Piranesi, Piazza Navona, 1773.

man have advanced parallel critiques of modern functionalism: the former because its practices of mechanical zoning are antithetical to an organic communitarianism; the latter because it retains a secret humanism that fails to engage the modernist transformation in the relationship between subject and object. In terms of the analogical pairings dear to their onetime sponsor, Colin Rowe, it is not entirely clear in this story who is Piranesi and who is Nolli. Given what Eisenman has written, he probably would like to play Piranesi in the remake, though he might get stuck with the role of Nolli, since the formal rigors of the planimetric appear more productive for him than the visionary cartouches and views that establish the atmospheric mise-en-scène for his counterpart and costar. Rather than assign prescripted roles, however, perhaps it is more accurate to suggest that there is a crossing of Nolli and Piranesi in both Krier's and Eisenman's work: an attempt to Piranesi-ize Nolli (Eisenman) or Nolli-ize Piranesi (Krier). In fact, Nolli and Piranesi are more particularly the personal brands of Rowe and Manfredo Tafuri, which suggests that what Eisenman and Krier are really doing in working through Nolli and Piranesi is recombining Rowe (and his interest in formal balance) and Tafuri (political critique), so that one ends up with formal-critique (Eisenman) and political-balance (Krier). In the Krier/Eisenman pairing, then, there is a genetic remixing of Rowe and Tafuri toward different ends. It is largely alongside this structure of dialectic or opposition that the critical project has unfolded over the last thirty years.

Disneyland in Reverse

In 1977, Rowe hatched the plot for *Roma Interrotta*, his scheme for returning to 1748 to recuperate the possibilities that apparently had been foreclosed by the subsequent experiences of modernity. Krier was in on the job,

Leon Krier, Piazza Navona, from *Roma Interrotta*, 1977.

having been assigned one of the peripheral sectors of the Nolli map, consisting almost entirely of one of Piranesi's embellished views of Rome. By Nolli-izing Piranesi, Krier's project reasserts the clarity of public space, since Krier's renovation of Piranesi presents one of several covered squares that aim to produce a new form of collective life in the city. This series of big-roofed monuments dispersed throughout Rome—vastly overscaled primitive huts—conjures some of the proliferating vernacular forms that John Hejduk proposed for various urban masques. In other words, there is a political model here, really a medieval model. The problem for Krier, and in some sense for Hejduk as well, is the industrial modern world and its political correlate, the (relatively powerless) city of liberalism. Thus, they have to move back to preliberal models, in which the subject is conceived not as an autonomous individual but as a member of a caste or social hierarchy. Since liberal individualism is understood as having eroded the possibility for public life in favor of a world of privatism, Krier returns to the moment when identity emerges only as the fallout of collective association. In other words, for Krier (as for Hejduk), disputing modernism entails rejecting the liberal city.

Interestingly, given his polemic, Krier reworks Piranesi's views with an almost modernist zeal: in the Piazza Navona, for example, the foreground is cropped out, along with almost all of the figures, the atmosphere, and the weather; the sun is redirected so that shadows can be erased and redirected to theatrical effect. Most significant, the ground plane is replaced with two different grids: a square grid that takes up two-thirds of the plane to the left and a smaller rectangular grid, with a vague resemblance to Manhattan, that occupies the right. On closer inspection, new figures, more or less one-half to one-third the size of Piranesi's originals, have replaced the eliminated bodies. This makes for a corresponding

Leon Krier, Blundell Corner Project, Hull, England, 1977.

Peter Eisenman, Church for the Year 2000, Rome, 1996.

Superstudio, *Continuous Monument (Coketown)*, 1969.

increase in architectural scale, a kind of Disneyland in reverse, where all built matter is now three times too big. In other drawings in the series, there is a similar erasure of figures, which produces a looming public space without a public.

The Big Roof

With regard to contemporary avant-garde and commercial practices, it is curious to note that Krier's renovation of Piranesi forms one moment in the protohistory of the "big roof projects," that spate of recent hyper-archaeologies that ranges from Bernard Tschumi's Le Fresnoy to Jon Jerde's Fremont Street Experience. With Krier, one might retrospectively say that you get the "Piranesi experience," the city under a roof. To that extent, rather than serving as a resistance to the market or the avant-garde, the big roof actually displays odd affinities to the split trajectory of an accelerated consumerism (Jerde) and a post-urban experimentation (Tschumi), and even suggests the secret correspondence between the two currents.

Within this countergeneaology, Krier's project bears more than a passing (if unlikely) affinity to the program of "total urbanization" evident in Superstudio's *Continuous Monument,* a series of collage-drawings that predates Krier's by about eight years. This provocative juxtaposition suggests that Krier's reflections on architecture and the city form part of the response and sensibility of the '68 generation, and are not simply a matter of style. In this configuration, the "debate" between Krier and Eisenman is not reducible to one of formal difference (neoclassicism versus neo-avant-gardism) but represents the diverse ambitions of two distinct architectural generations. In this regard, Krier shares certain strains or historical connections with others of his cohort, particularly Tschumi and Rem Koolhaas, all of whom, significantly, return to the Superstudio project of 1969.

Scaling Monuments

The urban monuments of both Superstudio and Krier are infinitely scalable and frequently reconfigured as domestic furniture or sculpture. Curiously, this scalar continuity or malleability infuses the work of both Krier and Eisenman. Eisenman's Cannaregio project of 1978 redresses the question of the monument through operations of scaling, producing a counter-monument that moves from the scale of a sculpture or object to that of a house to that of a museum, while serving as a hyper-archaeology for Le Corbusier's missing mat, the Venice Hospital project that had been proposed for the same site.

One early side effect of the technique of scaling is a loosening of the determinacy of figure and ground, a priority that was invented by Rowe and the Cornell school. Whereas the Nolli plan articulated the grain of public versus private, at Cornell the issue of public and private is displaced in favor of a more formal opposition between figure and ground, or solid and void, mass and space. Particularly since it is filtered through a gestalt optics, the city becomes seen through this other diagram that provides techniques to evaluate cities in terms of how good they are, how much they match the gestalt balance of figure and ground. If there is one thing that characterizes Eisenman's work throughout his career, particularly moving into the urban-scale projects, it is the systematic dismantling or confusion of that figure/ground priority. From the Rebstockpark project (1990–94) to the Church for the Year 2000 in Rome (1996) to the winning entry for the Canadian Centre for Architecture's design competition for the west side of New York (1999), Eisenman displaces figure versus ground through various devices—folding, the development of the interstitial, or the emergence of the "figure-figure"—to produce an alternative to the particular Rowe-inspired articulation of the Cornell school.

The Two Bobs

It is, of course, possible to establish an alternative contemporary genealogy for Nolli and Piranesi, one that is distinct from the Cornell trajectory and its ultimate involution in the work of Eisenman, who reconfigures the Nolli/Piranesi duo to produce the eruption of the event within the plan (that is, what I have characterized as the Piranesi-izing of Nolli). This alternative would include Robert Venturi, Denise Scott Brown, and Steven Izenour's *Learning from Las Vegas,* for instance, where Nolli and

Robert Smithson, *Asphalt Pour*, Rome, 1969.

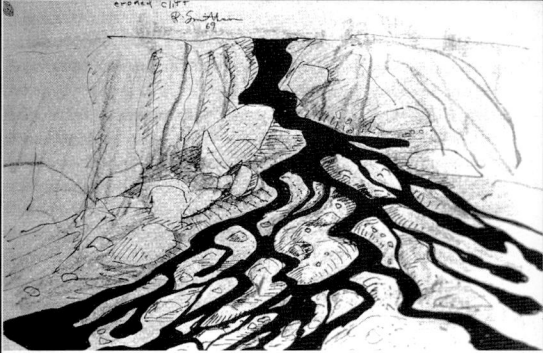

Robert Smithson, *Asphalt on Eroded Cliff,* 1969.

Piranesi make supporting appearances (for example, the postcard on the one or the marquee advertisement on the other) in order to demonstrate the priority of the sign over the plan (or over form or massing). In addition, the authors deploy an almost absurdist series of figure/grounds to describe the Strip, since no single figure/ground can adequately account for it. Here, it is through multiplication and speed that the idea of figure/ground breaks down, terminating in a figure/ground of all the automobiles on the Strip, where the city emerges—via the micrograin of these mobile incidents—as a hazy cloud with a vague shape but no definitive form. Finally, in the repeated juxtaposition of the Arch of Constantine and the Tanya billboard, Rome comes to be understood as a system of signs and graphics rather than as a monumental city of form and massing.

In addition to Venturi and partners, Robert Smithson was also seeking an alternative trajectory from the conceptual archaeology provided by the model of Rome. At a Roman quarry in 1969, Smithson orchestrated his infamous *Asphalt Pour* at the same moment that the research on Las Vegas was being conducted and the "Nolli" figure/ground was being canonized by the Cornell school. Here, at the ground zero of planimetric formalism, Smithson rejects the optical model of Cornell, replacing it with a thermodynamic model. In other words, *Asphalt Pour* demonstrates and capitalizes on the material (and significantly sectional or topographical) condition of entropy, an operation where black-on-white clarity ultimately dissipates to produce a field of even gray.

Just before *Asphalt Pour*, Smithson was also developing the possibility for a new form of (counter)monumentality in the exurban context of New Jersey, speculating on the unlikely thought experiment of Passaic as the "New Rome." One of the things that Smithson understands about Passaic is that, unlike New York, it appears to be full of holes. And so with Passaic, one gets the "holey" city, a city that cannot be mapped through figure/ground techniques. In other words, the two Bobs activate two alternative or virtual Romes: the Las Vegas–Rome and the Passaic-Rome. In grafting Rome to these two other posturban situations, there is a disciplinary shift from a preoccupation with monument (Krier's aggrandizement of Piranesi) and geometry (Eisenman's oscillation of Nolli) to one with infrastructure (Smithson) and graphics (Venturi). While the monument-geometry pair (that is, the work of both Krier and Eisenman) is tied largely to the problem of representation, to an optical-linguistic model of urbanism, and therefore a potentially *critical* model, the infrastructure-graphics pair instead solicits a *performative* model of the city.

From Roma to OMA

As a projection of the Venturi/Smithson combination for an alternative Rome, OMA's scheme for Lille, France, generates what Rem Koolhaas refers to as a Piranesian space, or a void, a hole much like those in Passaic, that reveals the circulation systems and signage. Similarly, OMA's first gesture for the McCormick Student Center on the Illinois Institute of Technology campus was to lay down a Pompeian carpet or wallpaper, where the lesson of the Roman city is located not in its monumentality or geometry but in its generic condition as background material that can be reorganized at will, utilizing the improvisational and expedient traits associated with infrastructure and graphics.

Film Rights

Some of you may have already seen the trailer for this talk. Despite its ostensible status as a musical comedy, *A Funny Thing Happened on the Way to the Forum* provides

Peutinger Table, second century A.D.

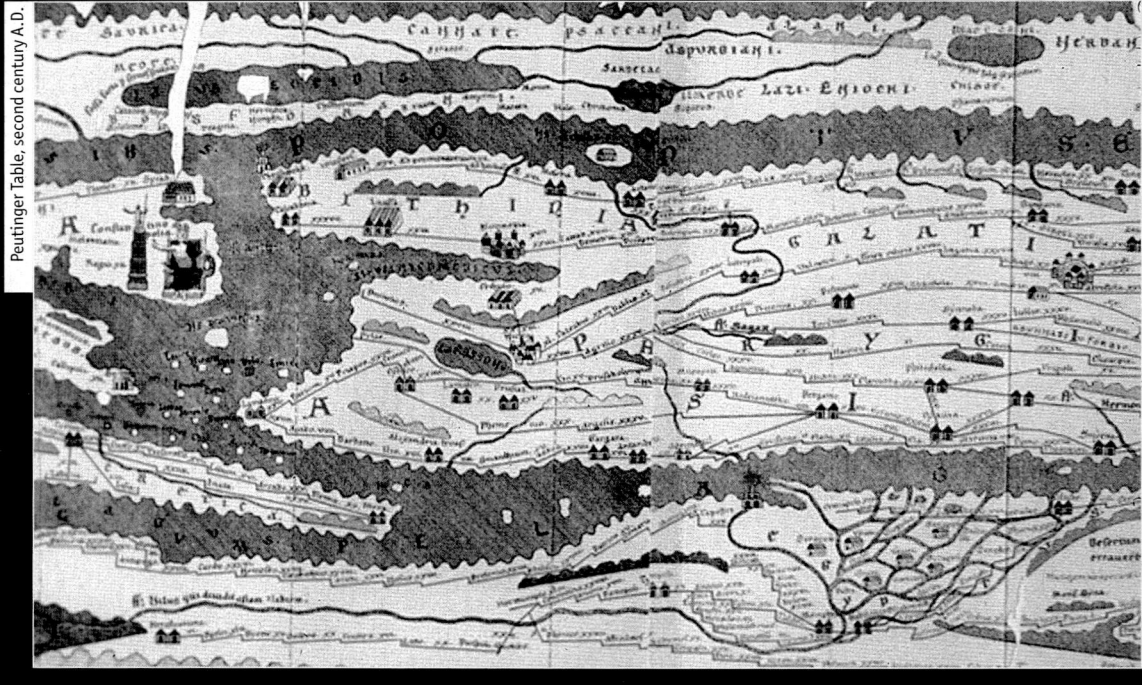

what many scholars consider to be one of the most accurate portrayals of everyday life in the Roman Empire. The streets are full of different sorts of bodies, animals, food, and goods; garbage and straw fill the openings and thresholds, obstructing and channeling a dense movement as horses, litters, pedestrians, and chariots collude and collide with one another. The built matter exists not so much as mass but as a continuous surface suffused with paint and graphics on the inside and on the exterior, as with Phil Silver's house of ill repute. This Rome, then, is not far from the entropy of Smithson's Passaic or the excesses of the Venturis' Las Vegas. It suggests that for my generation—or at least for that part of my generation represented here by Stan Allen and Sarah Whiting—there is a decisive shift from the critical oppositional or dialectical model of Rowe and Tafuri (or equally, of Eisenman and Krier or Nolli and Piranesi) to the ambient stochastic flow of Reyner Banham, evident in his documentary account of Los Angeles.

R/OS 2000

Apparently every generation has to reinvent Rome for its own purposes. With Venturi, Smithson, and Banham as distant guides, if not fellow travelers, a group of students participating in Harvard's "Project for the City" recently revisited Rome not as a particular place but as an operating system (R/OS 2000). In other words, the Roman system exists as a series of protocols for the production of the generic city, one that is much more involved with the devices of infrastructure and graphics than it is with those of monument and geometry.

Going back not quite 2,500 years but to the second century A.D., one uncovers two crucial documents of the Roman system: the Peutinger Table, which is a map or itinerary about a foot high and twenty-two feet long, and the text "Regarding Rome," by the rhetorician Aristides. The latter, which seems quite contemporary, largely celebrates the Roman accomplishment of turning the world into a single city. The Peutinger Table is a long scroll that documents a system of roads and networks with specific mileages and logistical stops along the way—a kind of convenient road map for early tourists. Its elongated form exaggerates east-west distances, so that the boot of Italy appears as a long strand in the middle layer of this horizontally stratified scroll. Clearly it is highly distorted because it needs to be carried around as an operating document for the empire. The message one gets from this, as opposed to Nolli, moves away from the Rowe version of figure/ground as gestaltist "face-vase" space toward the idea of "phase space," which operates more through solid/liquid relations, or states of matter. In other words, the Peutinger Table exposes a dynamic, materialist system where the empire functions as a series of flows that continuously scales down, beginning with the scalloped edges of the coast up to the turbulent figuration of the empire, which is rendered as floating in a sea of water. The flows associated with the Nile Delta in this second-century map become indistinguishable from Smithson's drawing for *Asphalt Pour*.

The most recent Roman forum is the shopping mall at Caesars Palace in Las Vegas, and in many ways R/OS 2000 runs *Learning from Las Vegas* in reverse: rather than using Rome to structure or explain Las Vegas, urbanisms like Las Vegas are employed to diagnose and project Rome, with the latter's now apparent manipulated landscapes, fluid infrastructures, endlessly reversible interiors, and saturated graphic fields. Las Vegas demonstrates the way in which economic development, whether implosion or building, starts to become its own form of spectacle through the extreme implantations of one ecology on top of another: future housing developments begin with the infrastructure of a golf course; a coin combined with a random-number generator results in a brand-new car; penguins spend their summers in the middle of the desert in a pool of water surrounded by misters that ring the trunks of palm trees. It is a marketable version of ecological and economic surrealism, one that announces the extension and insane survival of the Roman system.

Recombinant Projections

If it is desirable to imagine new modes of urbanism today, one may be advanced simultaneously from the possibilities offered by the contemporary metropolis and the impasses inherited from previous disciplinary configurations. It is no longer possible (or worse, interesting) either to revert to previous modes of the city or to avoid the political dimension of collective form altogether. In this sense it is useful to propose an unlikely remix. In other words, if Eisenman and Krier were remixing Rowe and Tafuri (in part via the surrogates Nolli and Piranesi), we might now be able to remix the genetic material of Krier and Eisenman themselves. I would suggest that this might produce a postliberal politics of the city, or what could be seen as a *political plasticity*. One aspect of such a program would entail ways to reinvent the plan. I do not mean the plan simply in the Nolli sense but rather the projective ambition of the plan, or planning. One way to think about this is through scenario planning, that is to say, the imagination of virtual futures that one then tries to inhabit. Bugsy Siegel, one inventor of Las Vegas, represents another form of this virtual futurology, having the epiphany that somehow, in the middle of the desert, due to certain invisible infrastructures and economies, a center for a new kind of lifestyle could emerge. The other figure on this deserted frontier of radical scheming is Wile E. Coyote, whose insane plans produce unanticipated effects. The project of political plasticity understands that the plan may well fail, but it remains necessary—that certain failure (chance, the accident) is part of its success.

Fast and Hungry

Colin Rowe once referred to the kind of shenanigans that Krier and Eisenman have engaged in since the mid-1970s as a kind of architectural "Punch and Judy" show. Perhaps, in fact, they are more like the Coyote and the Road Runner. I am not sure who is who, but given the Latinization that is a sign of assurance for one of them and the wordplay that is a near fetish for the other, one might reflect on the new worlds, not yet fully permissible to advance in the commemorative context of a silver anniversary, that become possible when *carnivorous vulgaris* meets *acceleratii incredibilus*.

POLITICS

How Eisenman Cut the Gordian Knot of Architecture: Looking at Giuseppe Terragni (1904–1943) from Afar

Kurt W. Forster

Nobody knows or remembers what Peter Eisenman looked like in shorts, traveling in Europe during the summer of 1961, or exactly what Colin Rowe told his student during their memorable trip. They were moving through the Continent, dutifully inspecting the landmarks of architecture that formed the subject of their studies and the substance of their professional culture. The results of such trips tend to be vague, difficult to gauge, and often slow in coming, but we do know what the visit to Como and Vicenza meant for Eisenman. What we know is not hearsay but stands before us in the corpus of Eisenman's work. That work bears the mark of a particular experience, which is intimately connected to but also quite separate from this "grand tour" of 1961. It was a personal experience and as such an incalculable, even irrational one, but it also gave rise to a sudden recognition that an architecture as he desired it already existed.

Eisenman's encounter with the work of Giuseppe Terragni and Andrea Palladio occurred well before he discovered in linguistics a "parallel universe" for architecture. The buildings by Terragni posed questions to which only *they* promised to hold any answers. Eisenman, a student from New York via Cambridge, England, was able to conceive of a "formal basis" for modern architecture or, in a word, of its intrinsic nature. What is intrinsic to it is precisely its capacity to act upon the world, to affect it in every possible way. Architecture thus assumed, in Eisenman's thinking, a dual quality: something that is like nothing else and that forever seeks a corresponding part. This is not the sole aspect suggesting a strongly sexual inflection in his thinking.

The grand tour on which Rowe led his students betrays an uncanny resemblance to the itinerary of that wordy reverend from Somerset, Thomas Coryat (1577–1617), who in 1611 published his widely read *Crudities*—"hastily gobled up in five Moneths trauells in France, Sauoy, Italy, Switzerland, some parts of high Germany, and the Netherlands." Like Coryat, Rowe visited the Netherlands, moving up the Rhine via Krefeld and Stuttgart to Zurich, then to Como and Mantua for the contrasting impressions of buildings by Terragni and Giulio Romano, and on to Vicenza and Venice, where the party was joined by Anthony Vidler. Rowe extended the excursion with forays into Umbria and Tuscany before descending on Rome. It was, in some ways, a trip backward into history, for early modern architecture prevailed in Holland and Germany, whereas in Italy, Palladio and Vignola came in for special attention. The baroque formed a divide between the periods of mannerism and modernity, as it did between Italy and the North. In Rowe's eyes, Palladio and Vignola proved inexhaustible subjects of "formal analysis," whereas the North offered a wellspring of modern ideas and objects to test them. Rowe introduced his students to the kind of architectural analysis he had learned from his teacher Rudolf Wittkower, whose studies on Palladio, proportional systems, and baroque strategies of display left their mark on an entire generation of English and American architects and historians of architecture.

By applying Wittkower's approach in a highly formalized fashion to modern architecture, Rowe became one of the most influential teachers from the 1960s through the 1980s. His analyses of buildings rarely failed to detect reverberations between "basic figures," as when he broke down Le Corbusier's 1938 project for an Algerian skyscraper into four different perceptual patterns. The key to these readings and to their motivation lies in Rowe's assertion that "the eye (or the mind) is compelled to provide further explanation."[1] He went on to compare the facades of recent American skyscrapers with Vignola's Villa Farnese at Caprarola, cautiously exempting them from any similarity in "function or structure (as generally understood), nor with the social context, technology, economics, or content; but simply with the manifestations which reveal themselves to the eye."[2] This latter-day phenomenology, as practiced by Rowe and Robert Slutzky, never led to a fresh perception of a building's "context" but forever forestalled it by sifting through impressions and proffering hypotheses about the ways the facades could be deciphered. Reduced to a purely phenomenal presence, the buildings were "appropriated" by a peculiar language of analysis. From these somewhat wobbly premises Eisenman initially hoped to develop a more systematic analysis of modern architec-

Giuseppe Terragni, Casa Giuliani-Frigerio, Como, Italy, 1939–40.

ture. At this time, he had not yet taken recourse in linguistic theory in order to break down the impenetrable presence of buildings. When Rowe asserted that "the eye (or the mind) is compelled to provide further explanation," he may have alluded to the fact that perception puts its objects under strain, or that his brand of "observation" could scarcely connect what can be seen to what it might mean. For such meaning to be adumbrated, perceptual schemes of Gestalt psychology are insufficient, for only the mind—notwithstanding the fact that Rowe put it in parentheses, letting the eye fend for itself—can discriminate among alternate figures and construct any meaning in their configurations.

Rowe called the things he observed by specific names. The distinctions he customarily introduced in his descriptions did not leave the objects of study unaffected. He located Le Corbusier—as indeed any architect he admired—in the land of individuality, Palladio and Vignola in the nether-region of "systems." These "systems" he carefully held free of symbolic connotations, as if to confine them to a perceptual limbo within which they keep on blindly permutating themselves. In fact, Rowe admitted that "comparisons, parallels, and analyses such as these could be prolonged almost indefinitely,"[3] but he never went beyond invoking theorems of Gestalt psychology and vague notions of an "intellectual style," or zeitgeist of the century. Rowe's schematic proliferations of grids and imbricated "figures," as he inscribed them, for example, on one of Michelangelo's projects for the facade of San Lorenzo in Florence, ultimately consigned every single component to a meaningless plurality of readings. Not only are the graphs entirely different from the facade, it is never made clear *what* they are. Undoubtedly, one could never compose such a facade from these schemes—hence, one is led to assume that such graphs must be an analytical device—nor can one recognize them as figures themselves. Instead they constitute "ascriptions," tracings that can have the purpose only of gradually softening up whatever resistance the original object may have had and thus break it down for refigurations. Rowe's landmark article of 1947, "The Mathematics of the Ideal Villa: Palladio and Le Corbusier Compared," makes explicit use of this stratagem: he stripped Palladio down to a matrix or "tartan"—an ultimate "Anglicism" about the Mediterranean—and allowed Le Corbusier to "modify," "deviate from," and "individualize" it. Asserting that "Palladio is concerned with the logical disposition of motifs dogmatically accepted," Rowe harked back to the "rediscovery" of Palladio by German art historians before and during World War I and paved the way for Eisenman's early interest in him. This interest has returned, as you know, and promises to lead to a perception of Palladio that is as far from Rowe's as it is from academic historiography. Rowe's graphic juxtapositions confirmed yet again Palladio's past importance, but they also set him up (in every sense of the word) as a "lodestar" for architecture *tout court*—as Goethe had celebrated him in 1786, before experiencing a sore disappointment.

Rowe first compared the plan of Palladio's Villa Malcontenta with that of Le Corbusier's Villa Stein at Garches. Not content with their tenuous resemblance, he "superposed" Garches onto the Malcontenta. The proposition was not just chronological but above all qualitative, for Garches, he surmised, had grown out of, and hence outgrown the Malcontenta. What made the comparison useful also made it superfluous, for Garches so completely absorbed the Malcontenta that it became its modern other. Perhaps more than any of his numerous observations, based as they were on flirting relationships, this one sprang from a manipulative eye. The European architectural tour of 1961 had clamorous consequences for the young Eisenman, but it may also have nudged Rowe to turn sympathetically toward a classicizing postmodernism. By 1987, in a kind of routine rehearsal of his thinking, Rowe dismissed Eisenman's Kochstrasse block in Berlin as "a pretty tough-minded pastiche of an Italy which many people just happen greatly to admire."[4] Admire, that is, not as "pastiche" but as what it was, as opposed to what it is said to have become in the "city of artificial excavation."

When, in 1961, Eisenman was unexpectedly overwhelmed by the architecture of Terragni, he also adopted some of the ways in which that architecture was rendered—both in drawings and photographs—during the 1930s. Eisenman preferred unshaded outline drawing and axonometric representation for his early houses of the 1970s, as did the Italian modernists in the 1930s. The return of the axonometric in Eisenman's analytical representations of both Terragni's and his own early projects and buildings makes the most of a type of view that matches, as no other, true dimensions with a synthetic view—that is to say, axonometrics are constructed on the premises of intrinsic consistency and extrinsic view. In contrast to Rowe's uniformly flat mesh of lines, axonometrics have only an analytical purpose, and it is precisely their unreality that makes them fit for their purpose. True, Richard Meier and others also excelled in line drawings—I remember how impressed Italian architects were in the 1970s when they recognized in them the ghosts of their own past suddenly come to haunt them. We should not overlook the fact that Eisenman's fascination with Terragni took hold at a time when the period of regime architecture was still kept under wraps, strongly denounced by the communist left in Italy, and barely rescued by Bruno Zevi from outright ideological condemnation. Nothing could have made it a more tantalizing subject for Eisenman His drawings, in contrast to those of Meier and Michael Graves, bore the stamp of diagrammatic rigor. Their wiry precision did more than submit to a graphic regime of the neoclassical stamp—for which Karl Friedrich Schinkel's plates furnished the most accomplished models and the best quarry for Meier, Aldo Rossi, and others. Above all, Eisenman's drawings bent visibly to the will of the architect.

In Eisenman's youthful experience, the architecture of Terragni seemed supremely capable of generating itself from a number of minimal elements by dint of their mere "displacements." What distinguishes Terragni's from others' geometrically regulated buildings is precisely this: their geometric matrix exists within them, but it is never uninflected, nor are its plural "readings" gratuitous. Instead of bringing ambiguities of Gestalt psychology to mind, the geometric schemes of Terragni suggest distortion, displacement, and even paranoia. This condition produces peculiar results. If we assume the matrix of the building to represent its initial, or original, condition, then Terragni's examples preclude that exact "moment of origin," for they have always already undergone some prior modification. The House for a Horticulturist of 1937 stands as a case in point: eight of the twelve pilotis are regularly disposed in pairs, marking the corners of three implied squares, but the other four, aligned in a parallel row, stand at a narrower distance. Throughout the house, minor deviations from standard lengths prevent pat correspondences from taking hold, and where approximate symmetries do appear, they usually remain just that, approximate. The same can be said for the "built-in" irregularities of the Casa del Fascio, where two bays are distinctly narrower than the regular grid would suggest, and many details, large and small, have been displaced from their standard positions. I betray no secret by citing Peter's favorite instance of such displacements, the curious fact that only when a window in the rear stairwell is extruded on its telescoping arms does its glass pane coincide with the back side of a cube within which the building could—but otherwise does not—attain a "perfect" geometric regularity. Not only is the opening mechanism missing today, but the very idea of telescoping a window pane out of its place in order to "return" the entire building to its "original" perfection may strike one as extravagant and, frankly, excessive. But that excess sets the measure for the distance separating this building from all the standard typologies invoked as its alleged source.

If our first impression of the Casa del Fascio were of a "formulaic building," we're in for a surprise. Everywhere, its constitutive elements—posts, walls, windows, mullions, railings, and so forth—elude diagrammatic confinement and obvious correspondence. In this respect, Le Corbusier's scheme for the Maison Dom-ino and the regular disposition of eight posts in several of Mies van der Rohe's buildings and projects from the late 1920s through the 1930s make for a telling contrast. Although Mies took liberties with the emplacement of walls and membranes of marble and glass, shifting them in space and differentiating them in material and visual effect, he never touched the cruciform posts. Such stark display of an elementary diagram, such deference for its tectonic significance could have only one purpose: it assured the persistence of an origin amid a fluid and shifting setting. Implying the presence of an "origin" within their buildings is what betrays the classicist in both Mies and Le Corbusier. By contrast, Terragni's architecture *blocks* access to its origins but opens up prospects for its own potential. Put another way, the *latent* state of its many internal ramifications calls for an exceptional degree of attention on the part of viewers. Only viewers can detect, intuit, or surmise the "moves" and virtual correspondences within the fabric of the building. This state of things generates in our perception, almost by itself, a "second fabric" within and without the actual fabric of a Terragni building. Partly emerging from mirrored correspondences, partly suspending such complementarities, our perceptions cumulate in a conceptual edifice that could be regarded as the "product" of all those inconclusive—or incompletely matched—correspondences. What might at first appear to be lacking is either supplied by our corporeal passage through the building or held in abeyance by it. Terragni's buildings, one after another, leave "open jaws" among their parts, produce slipped correspondences (*sfasamenti*), incomplete symmetries, and inverse correspondences. In a word, the liberty to make one thing differ from another—and the will to affirm as well as contain these differences within the whole—is a matter of supreme choice. Terragni is *systematic*, that is to say, he recognizes the rules he has established, but he does so only to the extent that these rules also yield *choices* rather than enforce a blind mechanical necessity. The price he has to pay is to forego origins; to accept absence, split identities, and "open jaws."

While Eisenman was writing his thesis at Cambridge and fixing his attention on Terragni, architecture back home saw a few figures emerge to prominence: Louis Kahn, Paul Rudolph, and Robert Venturi, to mention architects closely connected with Yale. However different their manner, Kahn and Rudolph reintroduced the building as an eminently physical object, as a container of its own idea. Such containment made the buildings' volumes swell, their surfaces stretch or crack, and their structures gain weight. There is no better place than Chapel Street north of High Street to gauge the changes that occurred between the late 1950s and the early 1970s, although my characterizations will have to be very schematic. With the Yale Art Gallery, Kahn sought to match an ancient Roman body with contemporary American technology for a Miesian concept of space (lateral stairs, plinth, sunken courtyard, movable partitions); with the Art and Architecture Building, Rudolph exacerbated the antiquity of his sources with his hankering after baroque effects; and with the Center for British Art, Kahn framed off the site with an almost Schinkelian exposition of a skeleton and syncopated fenestration. Common to all three is the adamant insistence on a physical identity between concept and building, swelling to a crescendo with Rudolph and only admitting subtle reservations with Kahn's Center for British Art.

Against this affirmative "reclamation" of presence, Eisenman's contemporaneous exploration of displacements, dislocations, and attenuations of a building's corporeal identity makes for a polemical contrast. What ancient Rome, German baroque, and Schinkelian parsimony did for the triad on Chapel Street, Terragni began to suggest for Eisenman's houses in Vermont, in Connecticut, and on paper. Particularly the latter, and especially House IV, started a train of thought that was to carry him further and further away from those early projects. Eisenman's trajectory suspended, even negated, the basis Kahn and Rudolph sought to establish for American architecture of the 1960s. When Eisenman characterized a key building by Terragni, the Casa Giuliani-Frigerio in Como, he also addressed this contrast and its broader implications:

> *While traditional architecture tends to be understood sequentially and as an accumulation of perceptions intentionally ordered by an architect, [Terragni's] Casa Giuliani-Frigerio raises the possibility of a different kind of perception, a perception of accretions contingent—as with other buildings—on the physical traversal in and around the building but, significantly, the traversal of a path that is never unique or hierarchical... Because the architecture itself no longer comprises a coherent image but rather a*

series of incohering fragments that initially appear to adhere to formal, structural, or compositional logics only to erode at the seeming point of reading, the experience of the viewing sensate subject is no longer the end result of a single—or even multiple—directed reading... [Terragni] comes closer to providing a disjunctive, disorienting, and possibly more active cognitive relationship between building and viewer—object and subject—than previous architectures.[5]

Over a decade ago, years before Eisenman finally published the text on Terragni I just quoted, Ignasi de Solà-Morales suggested that from these oscillations of reading, from the impressions an observer gathers in the course of experiencing a building by Terragni or Eisenman, there emerges a mental structure: "Behind these geometries which multiply their dimensions and augment or diminish their modulation is an energetic unfolding and opening out by means of which digression manages to establish a provisional supporting structure."[6]

Terragni's and Eisenman's structures do not actually coincide with their physical fabric; they hold themselves in abeyance and oblige us to supply what they withhold. As a result, a *dédoublement*, or doubling, occurs, inducing a constant oscillation between a building's physical elements and its perceptual manifestation. With a certain irony or inflection, Eisenman started long ago to sign his name with two pens—sometimes in gold and silver, sometimes in other colors—as if to make light of a burden or a liability. The liability is to architecture as something that can stand by itself, and *for* itself, only with difficulty. The only origin one can detect in Eisenman's architecture is that of an initial split, of a detachment of line from line, cube from cube, architect from architecture. From the gap opening up between them arises the "space" within which, in extreme confinement *and* complete abandonment, Eisenman can begin again. One other architect had already been there: Terragni. The difference may be that Terragni could only *imagine* his way out Eisenman could not. He had no choice but to *find* his way out.

1. Colin Rowe and Robert Slutsky, "Transparency: Literal and Phenomenal," pt. 2, in Colin Rowe, *As I Was Saying: Recollections and Miscellaneous Essays*, ed. Alexander Caragonne, vol. 1 (Cambridge, Mass.: MIT Press, 1996), 77. The original essay, written with Slutsky in 1956, was first published in *Perspecta* 13–14 (1971).
2. Rowe and Slutsky, "Transparency," 81.
3. Rowe and Slutsky, "Transparency," 97.
4. Colin Rowe, "Ideas, Talent, Poetics: A Problem of Manifesto," *As I Was Saying*, vol. 2, 346.
5. Peter Eisenman, *Giuseppe Terragni: Transformations, Decompositions, Critiques* (New York: The Monacelli Press, 2003), 296.
6. Ignasi de Solà-Morales, "Four Notes on the Recent Architecture of Peter Eisenman," *A+U* 232 (1990): 1, 127.

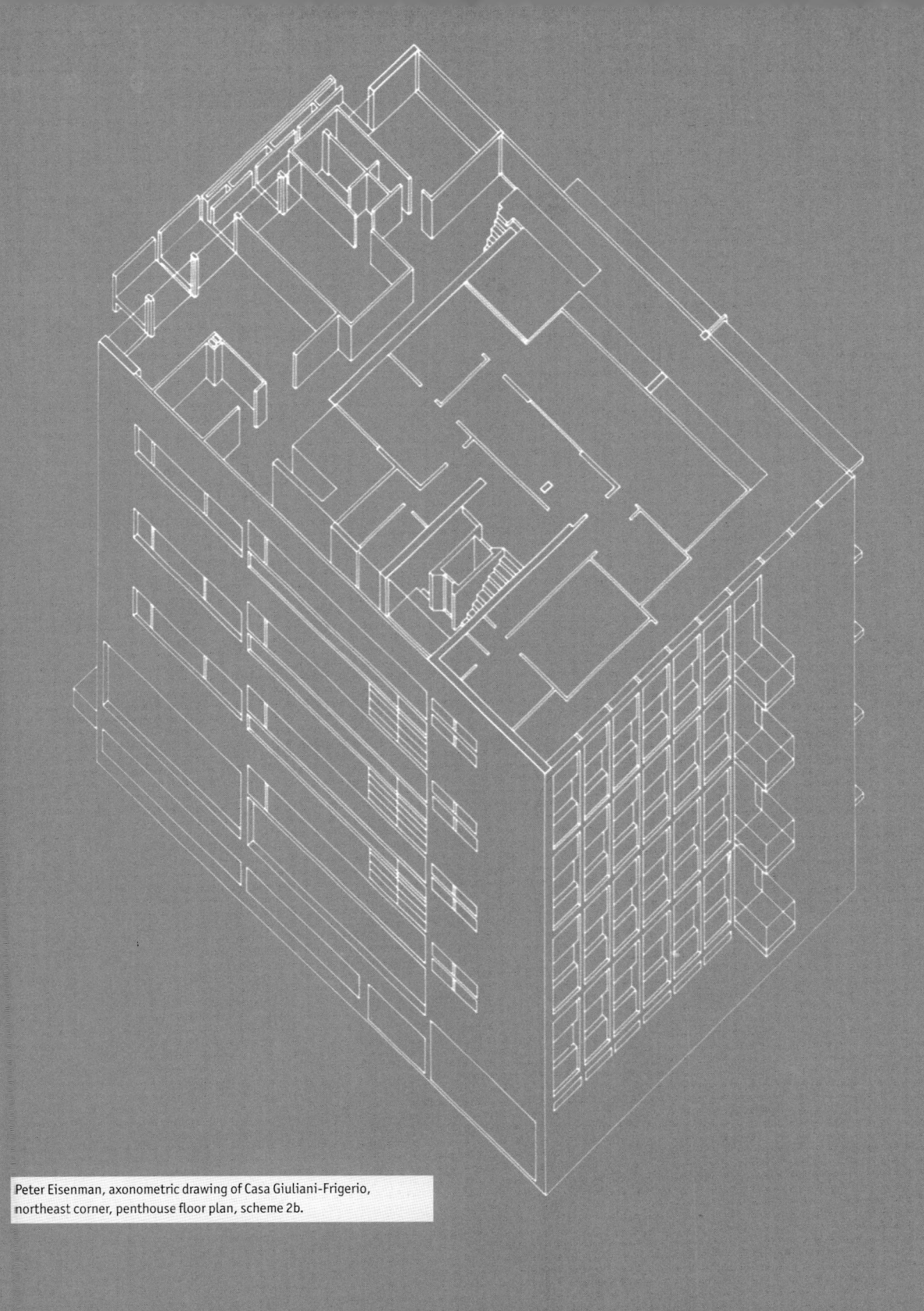

Peter Eisenman, axonometric drawing of Casa Giuliani-Frigerio, northeast corner, penthouse floor plan, scheme 2b.

On Albert Speer

Maurice Culot

I am a specialist neither in classical architecture nor in the particular case of Albert Speer. In the 1960s and 1970s, I had the opportunity to publish several essays on European architecture and town planning from the years between the wars; some of these works focused on Germany, the most remarkable being Leon Krier's *Albert Speer Architecture*. In this book, the first critical appraisal of Speer's architecture, Krier begins by drawing a line between the architect's work and his political ideas and connections to the Nazi regime: "This book cannot disculpate the crimes of a regime or a man. Classical architecture and the passion of building are its only subjects, its sole justification."

According to his critics, Speer is an untalented architect. Krier demonstrates that this point of view is not the result of serious analysis but is rather a confusion of political aims and cultural means. For example, Speer's detractors describe his architecture as oversized. To prove this wrong, Krier drew plans of contemporary buildings such as malls at the same scale as Speer's projects. The results speak for themselves: some existing contemporary buildings are even bigger.

The topic of this conference makes discussing Speer's work an arduous task. It is difficult to stay away from controversy since the very name of Albert Speer brings back painful memories. I am the first to understand that the atrocities of the regime to which Speer is linked make it extremely difficult to dissociate crime from art. As Krier writes, "There are humane reasons for equating powerful architectural images with tyranny, but this does not mitigate the fact that these equations are incorrect." I share his point of view and believe that when we become capable of dissociating a man's work from his political ideas or crimes, we can understand and prevent history from repeating itself.

After twenty-one years in prison, Albert Speer's 1969 memoir, *Inside the Third Reich*, drew attention to his case. Speer was sixty-four years old, had been close to the führer from 1932 to 1945, and was the Reich's minister from 1942 to the end of World War II. When *Inside the Third Reich* was published, many Germans of his generation were actually relieved. At the time, his life story showed that he was an

Great Hall of the Reich as seen through the Triumphal Arch, Berlin, Germany, 1934; model by Albert Speer based on the drawings of Adolf Hitler.

Albert Speer and Adolf Hitler inspect progress on the House of German Art, Munich, 1935.

Party rally, Nuremberg, 1934.

honest and naive technician, and that although he had worked for the Nazis, he was not a criminal himself. After all, given his very important status in the Nazi government, he should have been sentenced to death by the court of Nuremberg. On the contrary, he was treated quite kindly by the court and had every reason to hope for an early release.

In his recent biography of Speer, Joachim Fest writes:

After his release, Speer became sort of a symbol of innocence. His case seemed to prove that it was possible to serve Hitler, to be a high member of the Nazi government without being aware of its crimes and atrocities. Besides, in the late sixties, the positive aspects of national-socialism—less unemployment, social progress, highways—were often linked to the name of Albert Speer.

Today, we know that Speer's representation of his position is not true, and that the reality is more complex. Recent research, including Fest's, shows that Speer deliberately avoided mentioning in his memoirs and numerous interviews the criminal operations in which he was involved, such as the 1941 evacuation of Jews from Berlin. In fact, beyond the case of Speer, these recent discoveries have led many historians to question the attitude of the majority of German people of the time. As Peter Fritzsche wrote in *Germans into Nazis*, published in 1999, "It should be stated clearly that Germans became Nazis because they wanted to become Nazis and because the Nazis spoke so well to their interests and inclinations." Like the majority of his peers, Speer could easily guess that the Nazi government was perpetrating the racist crimes that were clearly defined in *Mein Kampf*.

After Germany's defeat in World War I, German people were disillusioned and disenchanted. They lost faith in their institutions and leaders, were sick of the rising urban insecurity, and longed for order. Into this context came the romantic and appealing project of a strong, rejuvenated Germany, brought about by an agitator who happened to be both a courageous soldier from World War I and a charismatic crank. The Germans knew that Hitler and his ideas were dangerous. They also thought it was only a question of time, that everything would return to normal as soon as order was reestablished. They forgot to take into account, however, that in some psychological circumstances, the human spirit can surrender to evil. Kurtz, the genius speaker and bloodthirsty madman from Joseph Conrad's *Heart of Darkness*, fascinates everyone who meets him, including Marlow, a staunch anti-colonialist, who surely knows how to distinguish goodness from evil. The barbarian horsemen who destroy an oasis of civilization in Ernst Junger's *On the Marble Cliffs*, published in 1939, bear an unmistakable resemblance to Hitler and his gang of murderers.

Speer was both a disciplined technician and an architect who could not resist the seduction of power; he was a monstrously perfect war criminal. Although Gitta Sereny ends her 1995 book *Albert Speer: His Battle with Truth* on an empathetic note, writing, "I understand how, after the end of the war, when Speer had to face an inner-battle, he finally took up with the moral standards that were part of him during his youth," she also argues that guessing is already knowing. Anyone can understand what a hazardous exercise it is to mention the artistic qualities of such a fascinating Janus. When Krier and I were working on his book, Leon—who had frequent discussions with Speer then—was worried about the interpretation of our intentions. We worked hard to make it clear that the passion for buildings was the sole justification for the book. Even so, when the book hit the stores, some people accused us of colluding with evil. You can easily understand how difficult it was to deal with these accusations.

Is it necessary to reopen the debate about Speer and his architecture? The world has undergone so many changes since 1980: ideologies have evolved, the USSR has given way to multiple republics, the European community continues to expand, and miniaturization and globalization have drastically changed centuries-old habits. This new context does not belittle the relevancy of Krier's analysis of the profound meaning of Speer's architecture. On the contrary, the recent success of ideas in favor of sustainable development and energy saving as well as the evolution of mentalities backs up the analysis. Krier's book is an important landmark. Writing a critical essay on Speer's architecture gave him the opportunity to explore important current issues such as the risks of an advanced industrial society that did not question its aims and means or reflect on its dark past. In Europe, the city is the living environment for millions of men and women. And yet, if today's industrial world creates magnificent, useful, grandiose objects, it is unable to create quality public spaces and cities.

On Classicism

My first indirect and unconscious contact with a new, postwar, industrial world was in 1946–47, when I was a little boy. My father, an engineer who specialized in metal bridges, had just bought a brand-new car, made in the United States, in which he traveled around a devastated Europe, sometimes bringing along his family. Much later I learned that the Kaiser-Frazer my dad liked so much was a subproduct of the American war industry. The iron and steel industries that had made tanks and big guns during the war had been converted to make automobiles.

By the late 1950s, I was a young man whose architectural studies were all about CIAM, Le Corbusier, Mies van der Rohe, Paul Rudolph, new towns in France and England. I studied with Frank Lloyd Wright and Paolo Soleri, but back in Europe I loved Peter Cook and Archigram's architectural fantasies. Christopher Alexander's essay "A City Is Not a Tree" opened my eyes: the modernist ideology in architecture was too simplistic, which was a mistake. In 1968, I began to be very active in urban conflicts, trying to prevent property developers and architects from destroying the beautiful architecture of Brussels and also collecting the archives of Belgian architects who worked before the war.

André Waterkeyn, Atomium, World's Fair, Brussels, 1958.

I met Leon Krier in the early 1970s, and a little less than ten years later I agreed to publish his book on Speer with the Archives d'Architecture Moderne. Around the time I met Krier, I had published a book about François Spoerry, the creator of Port-Grimaud, a seaside resort inspired by local southern French architecture. At the time, the architectural establishment despised Spoerry. Today, he is considered one of the founding fathers of new town planning. With the same open-mindedness and curiosity, I decided to publish Krier's book on Speer.

Many people were curious about the "Speer enigma," and I was too. How could such a well-educated man, a scholar, a disciple of the delicate Heinrich Tessenow, an intelligent artist and architect, a man whose father thought Hitler was a dangerous maniac, be a member of this murderer's gang? Today we know a lot more. Specialists have analyzed every fact known about Speer, from his relationship with Hitler—which could be compared to a love story, as strange as it may seem—to his techniques to remain sane in his Spandau cell. Even so, these specialists come to the conclusion that, as Hugh Trevor-Roper puts it, Speer remains a "frightening mystery." As Fest writes, "Engimas have not vanished because human nature is more irrational, more absurd than science would like it to be."

In his essay about the Roman philosopher Porcius Latro, the French writer Pascal Quignard writes, "Reason and civilization are a mask for the wild forces which they never have really parted from. Thru this mask, they even use these forces to expand." According to Quignard, Porcius Latro did not believe that human reason could be rational; on the contrary, it was everything but reasonable. As the Roman said two thousand years ago, "Rational thinking may be the most sentimental thing on earth."

According to Krier, classical architecture was implicitly sentenced more harshly at Nuremberg than Speer himself. Strangely, this was not the case for modernist buildings erected under Fascist regimes. Today, monumental classicism from the twentieth century (Speer, Piacentini in Italy, Henselmann in East Germany) is often associated with the crimes of totalitarian regimes. Just like Speer's pavilion, the Trocadero was unanimously acclaimed in 1937, though in Paris today it is often said to be a typical example of Fascist architecture.

The confusion between classicism and fascism and between regionalism and fascism is a European phenomenon. To understand how it occurred, we must go back to the early 1940s. As the war was raging, industrialists and politicians were making plans for the future: how would they reconvert the huge war industry in the peacetime to come? In order to achieve such a massive reconversion, to rebuild and develop the infrastructures of communication, restart industries, and build new housing, it was an absolute necessity both to drastically change the way those things were done before the war and to disqualify the building industry. The goal was to go from architectural quality to architectural quantity. To achieve this, it was necessary to wipe out architects' moral authority.

Detractors of classicism and regionalism could now argue that these architectural styles had been defended by Hitler in Germany and Petain in France. But as Krier puts it, Speer's and his colleagues' classical buildings were only a civilized appearance, a mask for a Nazi regime whose evil was rooted elsewhere. As early as 1944, the London-based journalist Sebastian Haffner understood this and wrote:

> Speer is the symbol of a new kind of manager, a man who plays an important part in all the belligerent states. He epitomizes the pure technician, the brilliant man who does not belong to a particular social class, whose only goal is to find himself a place in the sun. This kind of man reigns over the awful machinery of our times with total offhandedness. We'll get rid of Hitlers and Himmlers, but for the Speers, it's a much different story. No matter their individual life-stories, they are here to stay.

The mastery of vernacular and classical architecture and an extensive knowledge of styles are the qualifications that endow architects with authority. Modernist architecture, on the other hand, is an individual matter. Given that talent and genius are rare, the majority of modernist architecture is generally mediocre. It does not garner admiration among the public. The favors of the best modernist architects are the privilege of the powerful international snobbery, and even though numerous magazines show post–World War II architecture as part of the glamorous or trashy images of contemporary fashion, these images cannot hide the fact that this kind of architecture has, most of the time, ruined the structure of European public space, made ugly cities and countrysides alike, and created hostile suburbs.

Louis XIV's administration, supported by the architects, decided to put an end to the monopoly of jobs and corporations that, at the time, had control over the whole process of the art of building. Theories of architecture would now be edicts of the king's architects, who would obey him and adapt their style to the sovereign's needs and personal taste. The French Revolution put an end to this system, which had spread all over Europe, and politicians, technicians, and entrepreneurs promptly questioned architects' ideas. In order to protect their authority, architects soon came up with the concept of eclecticism, a method for building that relies on the capacity to adapt useful elements from the past to the present. Now they were the only ones who could coordinate an architectural project, which they themselves had made complex. They were the only ones who could combine building materials, the only ones who could solve complex construction problems. They no longer had the princes' protection though, which meant that they had to accept being questioned about their ideas and projects. This led to an important turning point: composition. In order to get the public's support, to create the essential social consensus, they developed architectural reviews. Competitions, exhibitions, and architectural magazines established a hierarchy among architects. In fine arts and architecture schools, this hierarchy soon became a means to single out the most talented students.

Before World War II, a similar eclecticism ruled European architecture. The drastic disqualification of large numbers of building workers—the construction workers, the ironworkers, the plasterers, the glassworkers, the cabinetmakers, the marble workers, the trompe l'oeil painters, the decorators—could not take place in such a context. Therefore eclecticism needed to be eliminated and replaced by a new kind of architecture.

This also explains why some modernist buildings erected under Fascist regimes (by architects such as Aizpürua in Spain and Libera and Terragni in Italy, whose architecture is among the favorites in art schools) were not banned. Because of the way they looked—with huge windows, white cement walls, metal or concrete frameworks, flat roofs, cubic shapes, and no ornament— these constructions did not seem to be in contradiction with the new ideals of massive production. I insist on "because of the *way* they looked," because the reality is different. These modernist works are actually so sophisticated that it is more difficult and costly to restore them than to restore a baroque castle. Le Corbusier's Villa Savoye, for example, has been almost entirely rebuilt three times since its construction in 1930.

Today, we can conclude that since about 1950, modernist architecture has not benefited from the moral anathema thrown on classical, vernacular architecture and architectural styles. Rather, European architecture as a whole has suffered from the massive disqualification of the construction workers, from fashionably in-then-out construction materials, from the absence of a structured architectural education, and last but not least, from the public's lack of consideration of architects and urbanists.

While the art of building and developing cities was a major preoccupation of Europeans in the nineteenth and early twentieth centuries—the Sittes, the Cerdas, the Wagners—after World War II, it came down to the construction of suburban housing and monofunctional zones. Not until the end of the twentieth century would some kind of tradition reappear, notably through the recent success of new town planning in the United States. In Europe, however, the modernist ideology is still very strong and thus prevents the majority of architects and administrations from taking an active part in the urban rebirth. In fact, it is mostly independent property developers who seem to do so.

About Size and Grandeur

"Why do men admire big things?" asks the French critic Quatremère de Quincy in his *Historical Dictionary of Architecture*, published in the early nineteenth century. According to Quatremère, grandeur is one of the main, if not the first, quality of architecture, and a crime committed with panache can arouse admiration. He argues that if monumental buildings (for example, the Pyramids) are at first striking, it is not a lasting impression, and boredom soon follows. Real grandeur, according to Quatremère, rests on the mastery of proportions:

> It is the variety and contrast between towers, domes and houses which gives a city its beauty ... We enjoy the most the sight of the works of Nature when their size makes us humble: the sensation of our microscopic dimension forces us to become wiser. In architecture, we enjoy huge buildings and projects because it makes us proud. We, being so tiny compared to the size of what we've built with our very own hands, love this idea of ourselves so strong and powerful.

In this light, Speer's fascination with the idea of supersizing is not so surprising. In 1978, in his foreword to Krier's book, Speer wrote, "The projects I have done for Hitler were an anticipation of the Reich's victories to come." For Speer, size and excess were not relevant arguments to condemn architecture. On the contrary, his projects were meant to embody a renewed pleasure of grandeur, like the Colosseum in Rome, the cathedral of Amiens, the Soviet Palace, or even the 1958 Atomium of Brussels. Like Quatremère de Quincy, he believed that the quest for greatness in size was one of humanity's natural aspirations. He compared his architecture to the achievements of the French architects of the Siècle des Lumières and of the revolution, because men of these times had such a high idea of reason that only supersized buildings could reflect their aspirations.

Despite his rhetoric, however, when Speer visited Saint Peter's in Rome in 1936, he was very disappointed: "The eye cannot perceive the real scale of the most colossal Christian church." In 1978, he began to wonder if, after all, expressionist architecture would not have been a better match for Hitler's ideas than neoclassicism, given that expressionism and Nazism had in common a strong sense of the irrational, deep-rooted violence, and agnostic mysticism.

This late reflection on the link between architecture and national characteristics can be compared to the ideas of the Hungarian architect Jozef Vago, who won the 1927 international contest for the construction of the Palais de la Société des Nations in Geneva. Vago, who took part in all of the major architectural competitions between the wars (the Chicago Tribune building, the Christopher Columbus Lighthouse in Santo Domingo), had studied extensively the problem of scale in public buildings. Vago was absolutely opposed to any kind of political nationalism, but he was a fervent defender of artistic nationalism: "One must clearly understand that nationalist policies and national identity are not the same thing at all." This idea was so important to him that he submitted a project to the Ankara Parliament architectural competition that had no chance of winning. Although he knew that President Atatürk wanted the new parliament to reflect his political project—the secularization of Turkey—he drew two minaret-shaped columns at the entrance of his version of the new government building. For Vago, a public building must symbolize eternity, not just the political decisions of a moment. He was convinced that in Turkey, just as in any country, the national identity would soon triumph in art, and tradition, which embodies the eternal soul of a nation, would soon win back its original place. He said,

> In that perspective, the minarets, which are specific creations of Turkish art, will no longer symbolize decadence, ignorance and corruption, but rather evocate the glorious centuries which they come from. By choosing to position them at the entrance of the parliament, my aim was to insist on my personal conviction that this palace, a symbol of a rejuvenated nation, must have a Turkish identity.

Vago's ideas are close to Jozef Plecnik's, but they mostly derive from cross-fertilization, a theory expressed by Odon Lechner, the founder of a peculiar nationalist Hungarian architecture.

In Italy, under the influence of Mussolini and the concept of autarky, architects derived their inspiration from Roman antiquity. For Speer, representing German national identity was not a priority. His architecture had to suggest the idea of Germany as the master of Europe. He was in exactly the same situation as Percier and Fontaine were under Napoleon.

In 1978, Speer wrote, "The question of size in my projects must be put in perspective with the Reich's political program and not with the criminal Nazi ideology." Hitler, who saw architecture as a powerful tool of domination, as a way to root his power, inspired the political program. The Berlin Assembly Hall was meant to contain two hundred fifty thousand people and its square one million more. Speer wrote, "People must be moved by their very own multitude." Speer insists that his architecture did not reflect an ideology but rather a political program. The program itself creates a new scale, which in turn must reflect its time. From that viewpoint, Krier does not condemn the size of Speer's projects but rather the way the architect intended to achieve them: drastic industrial processes that would have eliminated any possibilities for revival of the construction craftsman's trade for more than a thousand years.

Generally speaking, architectural supersizing and democracy do not go well together. Democracy is based on such principles as the respect of freedom, equality of all citizens, elections, negotiation, alternation of power. In a democracy, grandeur is not expressed in the monumental but rather in the quest for freedom, in social progress, such as social security for all, women's right to vote, paid holidays, and the right to go on strike. Of course, politicians will always dream about monumental buildings that symbolize their achievements, and architects will always be attracted by power. In France, President Mitterrand launched a series of *grands projects* that now suggest a series of records (the biggest opera house, the biggest library, the highest tower, the biggest arch, the most expensive glass pyramid) rather than anything grandiose. Yet at the end of his life, he told a journalist that he was most proud of the new gilding of the dome of Les Invalides.

I am a European citizen who values democracy. I think there is no better political regime. I also think that democracy and monumental, grandiose architecture do not go together. Hence, it is extremely important to preserve our heritage, for it has been erected under the influence of dark forces we do not wish back. Centuries ago, Roman temples became churches. Today, in Europe, obsolete factories are restored and transformed for new purposes. As Krier puts it, there was no need to destroy Speer and his colleagues' buildings. On the contrary, they could have been restored and used as a structuring basis for postwar German cities. Grandeur in architecture today is not a matter of size. Rather, it is found in the quality and the efficiency of the dialogue between the citizens and the architects.

LANGUAGE

Ex Nihilo Nihil

Demetri Porphyrios

Jean-Auguste-Dominique Ingres, *Enthroned Jupiter (Jupiter and Thetis)*, 1811.

Raphael, *Prophet Isaiah*, 1511–12.

More than a century ago, Matthew Arnold, in his essay "Hebraism and Hellenism," discussed the contradictions that shaped Western culture. The diverse traditions of Hebraism and Hellenism, he argued, have formed the Western imagination and can be said to be responsible for the ideas of the "good" that still inform our lives today.

The Hebraic tradition regarded as idolatry any representation such as we in the West have called art, since temples and effigies and paintings are but golden calves. The supreme obligation of the Hebrews has been to walk in the way of the Lord. The glory of the heavens was not a mere symbol of something else; it was the creation of God and an awesome reminder of God's omnipresence. Yahweh, speaking to Job, reminds us that man cannot rival the Creator: "Where were you when I laid the foundations of the earth?" And Job is abashed, for he is made aware that man can never by reason and craft become the maker. Hardly any Old Testament figure is allowed to create through reason. David is a singer and a dancer, and the prophets are ecstatic in praising Yahweh—who remains essentially unknowable. Man, in the Hebraic tradition, is not portrayed as *homo faber*. What counts is not how he reasons or what he makes but his devotion to Yahweh, the creator of all things under the wide stretch of the firmament. The awesome God of the Israelites spoke from the burning bush, remained unknowable, and forbade David to build a temple.

The Hellenic attitude toward man and his gods was very different. The gods visited the temples built for them by mortals and mingled in the private lives of men and women. Prometheus taught men all the arts, and they have since used their skills to create and enrich civilization. Hellenic thought is tantamount to philosophy—the love of reasoning and wisdom—but also to the quest for harmony and beauty. In their poetry, art, and architecture, the Greeks invented myth and symbol as expressions of human imagination.

In the Hebraic tradition, by contrast, God makes things by the power of his word and calls his creation good. Creation is brought into existence by God's spoken word, and it is an inexplicable act ex nihilo. In the Hellenic tradition, creation is

Rudolph Steiner, Goetheanum, Basel, Switzerland, 1913.

the mythical labor of the gods who reason and act with human minds. That is why the highest virtue for the Hellenic tradition is humanism, whereas the highest virtue for the Hebraic tradition is divination.

Western poetry, art, and architecture have been formed by these two ideas of creation. On one hand, creation (and when applied to mortals, creativity) is understood as the reasoned and inventive adaptation of precedent; on the other, creation is understood as inventive divination. It is in this very tension between humanism and divination that the genius of Western art resides. This tension has been responsible for the history of Western architecture; and it is this tension—of which Eisenman and Krier are prime examples—that we are here to debate today.

The idea of creativity as the reasoned and inventive adaptation of precedent leads us to the study of conventions, which, as we know, are based on analogies of form. Once we think of a building in relation to other buildings, we can see that a great part of creative design addresses the formation and transformation of conventions. All art and architecture is equally conventionalized, but we do not notice this because such conventions are always meant to appear natural and universal; otherwise, their role as the binding "cement" of society would be undermined. In fact, conventions can be studied best when one travels or when transformations occur in the history of culture.

The introduction of a two-dimensional sensibility in classical architecture during the Hellenistic and early Roman periods is such a moment. One witnesses here a shift away from the tectonic culture of fifth-century Greece and toward an atectonic treatment of the trabeated system. These are the first signs of a break between structure and appearance, which was to lead ultimately to the development of the facade as a symbolic image of the origins of architecture in structure and shelter. In turn, the facade was one of the greatest inventions of humanist architecture and reaches its highest achievement in Renaissance and baroque architecture.

The idea of creativity as inventive divination leads us to the notion of art as expressive vision. Though such a view has been a recurrent theme in Western art—especially when cultural breaks have occurred, as with the architecture of Byzantium or, much later, with romanticism—the notion of art as expressive vision is the defining feature of expressionism. This is an attempt to create a visionary world, liberated from the current language and values of society and expressive of the deepest levels of the personality. As Kurt Pinthus put it, expressionism strives "to free reality from the confines of life . . . by grasping it all the more passionately . . . with the intense, explosive power of feeling."

Expressionism discarded the trabeated-arcuated language of classical antiquity and looked for inspiration initially in the vegetal forms of nature, later in biomorphic plasticity, and finally in transparency as the fantastic, even sacral, evocation of industrialization. Vegetal form, the effulgence of plasticity, and crystalline transparency all aimed at giving form to the explosive power of feeling. They were all attempts at arriving at the modern "sacral object" through inventive divination.

Kurt Schwitters, Hanover Residence, 1924.

Peter Eisenman, Max Reinhardt Haus, Berlin, Germany, 1992-93: model.

Leon Krier, Atlantis project, 1987.

The investigation of imbalance, uprootedness, nausea, and intoxication was but a fleeting experiment in the 1920s, which proved, however, to be the uncanny precedent of deconstructivism today. Now we are traversing a period that may be described not so much as a battle of styles but as an abrasive coexistence of both classical humanism and deconstructive expressionism.

The vocabulary of disintegration, fragmentation, and disfigurement is presented today not as an instance of things falling apart but as a way of making things fall together. This deconstructive claim to order repudiated the very principles of humanist architecture: tectonics, typology, proportion, and figurative myth.

Deconstructive expressionists see themselves as prophetic visionaries who are called upon to explode conventions, which—in their view—have desubstantiated life. Their work is indebted to the expressionists of the 1920s, especially those interested in biomorphic plasticity. The work of deconstructivists has ingeniously captured the mood of a widespread uncertainty and has turned it into a baroque sensuous spectacle. We witness here a sensibility akin to Josef von Sternberg's wildly imaginative set masterpieces.

Faced with a world drained of meaning, Eisenman sought to fill the vacuum with subjective expressive energy. Without a social-ideological program, he insisted that he could mastermind an avant-garde that would discard function and context. In the place of function, use, structure, context, and history, Eisenman put forward arbitrary "rules" of composition and an invented context of fictional historical facades. Generally, the parody of a recent constructivist past and of an early-twentieth-century avant-garde was meant to highlight the inability of architecture to carry any significant meaning other than its own metalinguistic play. It is still to be seen whether Dr. Caligari was a megalomaniac or a compassionate therapist, but at its best, deconstructive expressionism, by risking absurdity, has given us the drama of startling vitality.

At the same time, deconstructive expressionism wants to establish modernity as the end to history. Hence, the Hellenic tradition is classified not only as "ancient" but as "archaic," which is meant to be a moral indictment of that which is worn out, spent, or merely quaint. We should realize, however, that the distance between a new work and the precedent that inspired it always points out the modernity of the work. There is no end to history; there can be no end to history. Originality, and thus the modern itself, exists in this distance between the new and the model, as the new employs itself within tradition.

Some would doubtless argue that the new has no tradition whatsoever. Jacques Derrida's *itérabilité*, for example, refers exactly to such an aimless "drift" inherent in all language. Language, cut off from any sense of home base, is a meandering away from any origins and from all cultural and social meaning. Neither the forms of art nor the words of language, however, are orphaned (as Derrida would have them), for they always acquire a parenthood in the context of the tradition that adopts them.

Architecture is always situated at this midpoint: architecture deals neither with origins nor with creation ex nihilo but with the distance traversed between the model and its present repetition. Architecture points to a dependence on the models that it conditionally overcomes so that it may formulate its own modernity.

Looking at the work of Leon Krier, we realize that the conception of an architect entrusted with a heritage must become once again as elementary to us as it was to Alberti. For Krier, classical humanism takes up the challenge of tradition and makes us see something more than we already know. Architecture makes us see the position we occupy within tradition by raising once again the questions of tectonics, typology, proportion, and figurative myth.

The classical today speaks of tradition in a modern voice, thus highlighting the human capacity for millennial continuity. The classical reaches across culture and time and heals the estrangement that humanism constantly faces. The classical is certainly the enduring and the timeless. But this timelessness always takes the form of modernity.

The Art of Listening to Architecture

Mark Wigley

I would like to start by saying that I agree with Demetri Porphyrios on two points, but only two. First, the claim that deconstruction is a claim to order, not a claim to disorder, that it is a new way of paying attention to how things are put together rather than a description of the way things fall apart. I agree. This is extremely important. If there is anything radical to deconstruction as a way of thinking, it is precisely that through the seemingly paradoxical complications, through the apparent disruption, through the gaps, that order surprisingly but persistently arises rather than collapses, and that order is therefore to be respected even more than its defenders insist. This is the whole point, perhaps the only point, and a big thing to agree on. The second point of agreement is that so-called deconstructivist architecture is, or should we say was, historicist. Indeed. I am unconvinced that there could be a non-historicist architecture that was in some way wholly of its time, that is to say, new, or at least much more new than it was old, so that one felt the newness much more than one felt the reference to the old. Far from abandoning history, deconstructive thinking is all about unearthing old ghosts, tracing the way that systems are inhabited by the very things they appear to have left behind. It seems to me that it is a long time since architects tried to appeal to radical newness with a straight face. Maybe there are some younger architects who have done so in recent years, but their work clearly echoes and extends the experiments of previous generations, and now they are starting to proudly place themselves within this longer historical tradition. How could architects speak a language that they do not already share with the people they are talking to? On every other point, there is not so much agreement between us, I'm afraid. But at least it is a start of a conversation.

About what? Language, of course. The official theme of our panel. But what is the theme of the conference as a whole? What is the context for our discussion about language? Bob Stern invited us to talk about Peter and Leon. By the way, that is how we talk in architecture, with first names, as if we are all close friends or family. Such intimacy is normal for people spending a couple of days together like this. Architects also have this wonderful way of feeling close to people who are not in the room or have never met. Even dead architects are welcomed and discussed as if they are in the room. We are constantly talking with all the architects who have preceded us. Names keep flowing into the room as the conversation proceeds. But what is this conversation about, this event that seemed to be founded as a kind of disaster, the construction of an ugly head-on traffic accident between two ancient opposing points of view? As a student said yesterday, "Why would I go to a conference about dinosaurs?" It was then that I realized that the event would be a success. After all, dinosaur movies have been such a hit in recent years.

Looking around the room, this might really be a conference about bow ties. Bow ties, like Leon and Peter, have long been thought to be an endangered species, almost extinct in an age in which the absence of any kind of tie is the official uniform of the artistically or intellectually

Walter Gropius, Le Corbusier, Marcel Breuer, Sven Markelius, 1958.

119

Peter Eisenman, 1998.

minded architect. But there are a surprisingly large number of them here. The bow tie is alive and well at Yale. This little accessory was for a long time an important thing for architects and lawyers, and I have always wondered what the connection is. Architects pretend it is because a regular tie will fall down on their drawings; I am unsure what the lawyer's defense is. But surely what the lawyer and the architect have in common is that they both talk a lot; they have to talk. There may be something about the bow tie and talk. We have watched the bow tie bouncing from under the moving lips of Gropius to Eames to Rudolph to Eisenman. We could do a whole history of the bow tie fluttering like a butterfly from architect to architect until it ends up in this room. Maybe some kind of secret knowledge is released from the inside of the knot, guiding the words of the speakers. We could even have a Ph.D. dissertation on bow ties, starting with the one of Gropius carefully preserved in the Harvard archives and moving on to the key historical moment when Marshall McLuhan proudly declared that his was fake and pulled it away from his neck to reveal the plastic structure. We could ask Peter, whose work started to appear in the very same years, serious questions about his bow tie. Is it real? Simulated? A commentary on postclassical anguish? A knot somehow capturing the whole drama of the Hellenic versus Hebraic traditions? Does it displace or rebuild the person who wears it? In so doing, we find ourselves echoing precisely the argument of Adolf Loos, who challenged Joseph Hoffmann by discrediting his bow tie as a fake. Perhaps our history could start with those wonderful images of Mackintosh and his enormous flouncy bow, his flowery artistic tie capturing the ambitions of Art Nouveau that would eventually give way to the clean, reduced, black managerial bow of Gropius at the Bauhaus, though that too would widen and soften and become colorful—as he migrated to Harvard—before mutating itself a few times while making its way to Yale and to this conference here.

But I am sure you do not take me seriously. I am sure you want to dismiss the bow tie as just a decorative element. You don't see it as playing a structural role in the architect's discourse. Yet such seemingly secondary details are always a serious matter for the architect, like the seriousness of a decorative molding in a building: its original purpose, like that of the tie, is to hide a gap. The bow tie has precisely to do with the architecture of the body, in this case the architect's body. The architecture of the architect then. Who would suggest that architects are not obsessed with the way they look and the look of their colleagues? Aren't we here to say how Peter and Leon look to us today? Isn't Leon's trademark off-white suit just as much a part of his polemic as any published concept? Isn't it the case that students of architecture all over the world could draw what Peter and Leon are wearing today without being here? Isn't the way architects systematically construct themselves as architects, the performance of the architect, inseparable from what they are saying, just as any medium is inseparable from the message or sometimes becomes the most important message? It is precisely when taking an architect seriously that we should take seriously all the seemingly nonserious, or even pathetic, details that may play an unforeseen structural role.

But perhaps you are right. Perhaps this is not a conference about bow ties after all. Perhaps the real purpose of the conference is, as advertised, to celebrate two polemical architects—also an endangered species, yet a species that is alive and well in the room. There are many polemical figures present, people who can tease you into seeing the world differently, speakers who are a pleasure to listen to. It is always important to listen, even to last night's bow tie lecture—a kind of Martha Stewart view of architecture. The speaker was careful not to provide a glimpse of insight into his subject. This was to be expected. After all, the routine anti-intellectual tone of the lecture, speaking of tradition, is part of a long anti-intellectual tradition that has culminated in the current regressions in Washington. Not to be taken lightly. Surely, Mr. Kimball—not an architect so we should not use his first name—said exactly what he was expected to say. I share his deep interest in what is going on in the university, but I was struck by his evident lack of affection for architecture and therefore could not get interested in his particular opinion of architecture in the university. No one would expect him to share the love of architecture that we architects have, an endlessly foolish love no doubt. Indeed, it is perhaps necessary for social critics to point out that architects are too hopelessly in love with objects, and are therefore too irresponsible, as presumably are people who are in love. But to be entirely without affection for architecture itself is a bit of a problem in a conference about architecture. There was no talk of love last night, the word we use when we cannot be precise, when we cannot control the situation, our word for opening up to something outside ourselves, something we cannot predict or fully understand. To love architecture is to love what you do not know about it and embrace the thought that it could, at any moment, turn on you, surprise you, frustrate you, or entrance you, like any other lover. To love architecture is to endlessly try to understand something that escapes understanding. That is what an architect is, somebody in love with the fact that they do not know what a building is. The architect is the person for whom a building is a question mark. We know more about buildings than anyone else, but we also know that we know so little. We have been talking about buildings now for more than 2,000 years, and we still have not figured them out. I think we take pleasure in not having a definitive answer to our questions. It's why we are willing to spend long, beautiful fall afternoons foolishly talking on and on about it in rooms like this one.

It is in this spirit that we might try to think about language here, try to grasp the linguistic dimension of loving architecture. Let's start with the obvious. As architects, we love lines. That's the beginning of the affair. Get a line, any line, and the architect starts to talk the day away. It could be a detail, surface, texture, or space. But first a line, like the big fat one drawn right through the middle of this conference, literally bisecting the posters and brochures, the line between white and black, between enlightened tradition and angst-ridden doubt, between classical certainty and avant-garde uncertainty, between reassuring order and destabilizing disorder, between known precedent and unknown future, the line between Leon and Peter, a line that, by the way, seems to become sharper and sharper as the day goes on. If you look at the poster, it is clear that I belong to one team and Demetri belongs to the other as part of an ever-escalating tournament. It is as if all the speakers are meant to attack each other in public for the amusement of the gathered throng, pair after pair taking each other apart and their remains being cleared away until at last the heroic gladiators themselves will arrive, having killed all of their disciples by encouraging them to foolishly take part in this conference. Now the gap between these two gladiators seems far too big to be bridged by any kind of civil debate, too big even to fire missiles across it. If you forget for the moment what seems to be the yawning division between classicism and the avant-garde, one side seems to be about city planning and

Hans Namuth, portrait of Walter Gropius, 1952.

the other one not. One asks, "What is the appropriate code?" and the other doesn't even care about the question. In a sense, no exchange is possible, not even the beginning of a discussion.

And yet these two quarreling friends of ours, these two family members, are not so different in the end. To quickly point to an obvious symptom: both are equally strict about rejecting the so-called radical architecture of the 1960s and early 1970s. That is to say, both emphatically detached their architecture from technological expressionism, electronic pop culture, reprogramming, infrastructure, systems theory, radical mobility, operations research, media interfaces, drugs, sensory intensification, and so on. A vast terrain of experimentation is dismissed. This is a very particular rejection. If we did a little homework we could locate the point of rejection, looking again, for example, at *Design Quarterly* of 1970 on conceptual architecture, in which the radical work of Archigram, Superstudio, Haus Rucker & Co., and so on is introduced by Peter Eisenman with a textless set of footnotes. In that moment he is close to this group, alongside them, but even then his lonely footnotes start to establish a polemical distance. On the side of Krier, we could look at the close relationship between himself, Adolfo Natalini, Peter Cook, and Rem Koolhaas, as would become evident at Günter Bock's Städelschule in Frankfurt. With some research we could monitor the moment he was blended into that milieu in order to see more precisely his disconnection from it, as marked by his scathing 1975 review of the book *Architettura radicale* or, to put it more correctly, his lightly scathing review, more scathing than scathing because the work had not even aroused real anger on the part of the reviewer. He simply suggests that the book is just a demonstration of why one should not bother thinking about any of these architects. In the end, the approach of Eisenman and Krier will be to act as if all of that architecture, all of those remarkable experiments, had never happened. You can go through all the pages of *Oppositions*, for example, looking for even a trace, a passing footnote, pointing to these suspect practices. Why do these two strong, thoughtful architects want to act like so much work never happened? Presumably to make a space for themselves, to clear a space in which they could stage their gladiatorial combat. In the same way that it was demonstrated so well today that Leon Krier removes the extraneous elements from his images, extraneous architects and ideas are removed in order to allow for the showdown between classicism and avant-garde, a death match that will be endlessly restaged, a bloody road show that has arrived today in New Haven.

These two rivals are therefore occupying exactly the same space. When a space is cleared for occupation, an architecture is already constructed. If you construct and occupy the same space you have to share a certain amount of language. You have to agree on what the rules of the combat will be, and therefore you are very close. In the background, you might faintly hear electronics beeping as experimental architecture goes through all its permutations, but it is way off in the far distance. You find yourself looking into a small defined circle, as we are today, a circle in which the new-new fights against the new-old, the new anti-urbanist versus the new urbanist, both cherishing the word *new* but flipping it in opposite directions. There is the rule that the rules can never change for one gladiator and the rule that the rules have to keep changing for the other, and that that is what they are going to fight about. Now it is obvious that in this particularly arcane form of combat, both teams depend on each other. In a sense, they are simply two matching brands. Two rival products pushed by two pitchmen, front men locked together in what could only be a pseudofight, since so much negotiation has to have gone on to agree on these obscure rules of combat that by the time the fight begins, it is really a kind of decorative gloss, an ornament, like a bow tie covering the fundamental agreement that got the two of them together in the circle. They even draw pictures of each other. At their first meeting in 1977 at Princeton, one of them does the poster for the other. Krier devotes great care to an image of Eisenman for an exhibition publicizing House X. The same image appears a year later when *Oppositions* publicizes Krier and Maurice Culot, and eventually the same image is used at the end of *Houses of Cards*, a book in which Eisenman tries to explain his whole sequence of experimental houses.

Louis I. Kahn, Yale Center for British Art, Yale University, New Haven, Connecticut, 1969–74.

What we are talking about here is a couple. The affection between the two was first declared in 1977 at Princeton, then six years later in an interview for *Skyline* magazine, then exactly six years after that in *Architectural Design* with the "My Ideology Is Better than Yours" issue, and now exactly twelve years later. I have a feeling that there must have been an event six years ago of which none of us is aware, which is surprising, since the level of publicity has gone up each time. The first time they got together was a small event, and do we know that it really happened? On what basis are we deciding that there was this 1977 meeting they refer to? It was an unpublished conference. Then there is the *Skyline* interview, published with pictures of them sitting around a table. Then the special issue of *Architectural Design*, now with color pictures. Today, there is the exhibition catalog at Yale, with a web site, the book of this conference, and who knows what else. In a sense, what is going on here is just a further symbolic intensification of the relationship between these two lovers. This family gathering is something like a wedding. Or to be more precise, it is the twenty-fifth anniversary of a wedding, a renewal of the vows. The bride, no doubt, will wear a white suit. Of course, this means that the bride's family has to pay for the event, so we have to thank their step-dad, Bob, for being the gracious host. But before making one of the required bad speeches at the wedding, what side of the aisle am I supposed to sit on, what side of the line dividing the room in half? Obviously, I will sit on the side of Peter Eisenman. I know him, like him, and respect him. Also you get to see more if you sit on the dark side. At first you see nothing, then your eyes become extremely sensitive. It is paradoxically harder to see when you sit in the light, the full light of the classical tradition. You only see yourself, even imagine yourself to be the source of the light. The advantage of sitting in the dark is that you can see the one sitting in the light, and can maybe criticize, or attack, or just think. It may be harder to think when you are at the center. So I sit on Peter Eisenman's dark side, and speak here as a friend of the groom, but I will not defend him. That is probably why I belong on his side. One of the characteristics of the people who sit on the side of the light is that they will defend each other loyally, talking about each other's brilliance. They will act like a family or a certain kind of officially happy family. The dark side is the side of the people who misbehave. You do not defend anyone else on your own team; you earn your spot on the team by not being a team player. Anyway, I have no interest in falling on my sword for the nonclassical. Peter can take care of himself perfectly well. More precisely, the two of them can take care of each other.

They are, as it's said, a charming couple. The charm of Peter is that he is so extraordinarily inefficient. He is an absolute model of inefficiency, smothering his projects and colleagues in words, a kind of baroque excess of words, concepts, and drawings, always trying to irritate people into some kind of reaction, always trying to shake the tree to see what will fall out. Don't be fooled by the bow tie. Nothing in the room or in the discourse is safe. Peter is an unmatched provocateur, and is therefore absolutely essential. It is hard to imagine architectural discourse in recent years, indeed for many decades, without this level of relentless intelligent provocation. So easy to make fun of, as was done last night, but so difficult to emulate. The charm of the partner, Leon, is that he, on the opposite side, is so relentlessly efficient. One slogan per drawing. One drawing per idea. He even thinks in capital letters like Le Corbusier. In early drawings, he refused even to draw a complete line. He dotted the edges of the buildings—that would do to define them. Always the absolute minimum use of resources. And notice in those early drawings that there is no surface, no materiality to the buildings. They are strictly modern drawings, all about the efficiency of communication. An elegant writing style, it should also be said, combined with a kind of machinelike manifesto efficiency in the name of an argument that will attack exactly that—machinelike efficiency. So a kind of efficient modernist argument against modernism. Throughout all of this, he is trying to sustain a sense of clarity in stark contrast to those around him, but probably in the end he is just acting as another well-dressed lawyer, drafting mechanical rules legislating an all too safe lifestyle. So we are back to the lawyers again. One thinks, for example, of other elegant writers in architecture, like Alois Riegl, who were originally trained as lawyers.

So, a well-matched pair, and I am not going to speak for one side of the couple or the other. We should just be happy for them to reaffirm their bond in public. Rather than analyze their unique contributions to architectural discourse, I want to insist on their similarity and quickly question the basic conceptual opposition that allows them to so famously appear to be on opposite sides.

In my view, the classical versus avant-garde distinction is a red herring and has been so for a long time. I, for one, am perfectly happy to embrace the so-called classical tradition precisely because it is riddled with inconsistencies, confusion, and transgressions, which may not be true of the avant-garde. Actually, you can only transgress within the classical tradition, a tradition that has been, for thousands of years now, one of intense and endless debate. It is all about certainty, but it has never itself been certain. The rules in the classical tradition are only established so that a genius can demonstrate genius by breaking them and making the work even more beautiful. That is to say, there is a kind of doubt about the rules built into the very discourse that celebrates the rules. The entire tradition stages a dynamic between imitation and innovation. Architects have argued endlessly about the meaning of the rules. It was a thrill when I was able to go to the top of the famous columns of the Parthenon a few years ago during its restoration, to stand way up there where only the original builders had stood before, and to hang off the scaffolding in a strong wind to touch the traces of the original decorative paintwork that somehow survived the raging fire after the devastating explosion and the centuries of exposure to the elements. To go, that is, to the heart of the central paradigm of the classical tradition and hear the expert who is lovingly taking care of the building, restoring it fragment by fragment, describe with great pride the various ways in which his building breaks almost all of the very rules for which it acts as a paradigm. The classical tradition is never fixed.

It is dominated by disagreement. If you really want to find people who disagree, head into the classical tradition. Paradoxically, that tradition maintains an intense sense of modernity. When continuing the ancient struggle with the rules, there is always the feeling that your struggle is the unique struggle of your own day. In the avant-garde tradition, a revealing contradiction in terms, there is a too-smug reassurance that shock is the name of the game, which cannot be so shocking in the end. The very expression "avant-garde architecture" is probably a contradiction in terms. The word *architecture* has meaning in our culture only inasmuch as architecture has offered reassurance by resisting time, a dream exemplified by the classical tradition with its supposedly eternal geometries. Inasmuch as architecture can seem to escape time, it can act as a framework, or a mirror, allowing the unpredictable flows of daily life to be exposed, offering the thought that there is an order beyond the disorder. Anyway, the so-called avant-garde tradition in architecture is almost one hundred years old, already officially an antique. Modernism is the next antique. It's highly likely that there has never really been an avant-garde in architecture. Its advocates seem far too certain about the need for uncertainty. Anyway, the myth of the avant-garde has always had classical temples as its reference point. Again and again, the Parthenon pops up as the key. This is unsurprising since the cult of transgression requires the idea of the classical to give itself force. At the same time, the classical tradition is so much stranger than its most ardent promoters could ever acknowledge, so much more perverse in its complications.

All this is just to say that the debate between the classical and the avant-garde doesn't really seem to be a debate to people of my generation, which is why we find ourselves here for an event like today's, like ungrateful children who take advantage of what we have been given by turning against the people who gave it to us. We are not so interested in this struggle between two forms of nostalgia for things that architecture never had, two choices of how slow architecture should be. Very slow or just a little bit slow? Echoing the sixteenth century or the 1920s? The whole classical versus avant-garde distinction is a distraction. The only real difference, perhaps, is just on that finer point between doubt and certainty, between alienation and comfort. If you look at the writings of Leon Krier and Peter Eisenman, you will repeatedly see that they ultimately disagree only on this exact point. So the line drawn through the conference is really between comfort and alienation, a choice that exists within the classical and within the avant-garde, rather than between them. And since this is the panel on language, the question becomes, what does it mean to be uncertain or alienated in architectural language? Or more important, in reverse, what does it mean to be certain or comfortably at home in architectural language? It is easy to demonstrate that language is always riddled with insecurity, paradoxes, and so forth, and that architects are actually in love with these dilemmas. Yet it is also easy to show that language is inevitably more stabilizing than those who promote instability would like us to think, that you are locked into a very tight geometry once you start to talk. This is again exactly the point, that order arises through and depends upon disorder, rather than being dissolved by it.

The opposing views structuring this conference are therefore both inadequate. If you associate language and architecture in order to associate architecture with stability, or if you identify architecture with language because language is unstable, you share the basic understanding of architecture's basic representational operation. Both, that is, are committed to a certain language view. The classicism versus avant-garde debate is therefore not about language at all. Indeed, architects do not have a choice about language. Or to put it slightly differently, to choose to be an architect is already to have chosen language. We do not have the physical environment—buildings—and then the various attempts to describe it as a language. Rather, there is only the ongoing attempt by architects to persuade people that buildings are a form of language, that buildings themselves speak. Architecture in its most ordinary definition is articulate building, building that speaks. It is not simply that buildings are seen to act like a language. Rather, architects describe buildings literally as speaking objects. In this sense, the whole point of architecture is to talk and the role of the architect is to stitch words to buildings, which they are extremely good at doing through a kind of ventriloquism. Drawings, models, and buildings are passionately described as representing certain ideas in the hope that after a while people do not have to hear the description, believing that it is the building itself that is talking, believing when walking down the street that they hear buildings whispering this and that about themselves and the world, unaware that the buildings might have been invisible, silent, not even thought of as architecture, if there had not been so much talk. There is no architecture without talk. Words, words, words. All architects talk, have to talk. The only issue is how they talk.

To talk about language here, we have to talk about how the architect, as a unique species, talks. Before addressing the way architecture might be a form of language, we have to look at the very specific language applied to it, that of the architect. We teach our students how to talk. We do so much more effectively than we teach them how to draw. In fact, since Walter Gropius, it is entirely possible to be an international architect of great influence without learning how to draw. In some circles, it is considered a serious advantage to not know how to draw. But to not know how to talk is to immediately have left the discipline. This special form of talk needs to be analyzed at length, but for now I just want to quickly address the way we hear it.

If architects have a unique form of speech, what is it for us to listen? How do we listen in architecture? This is the side of the conversation that is usually left out. For example, we speak of "talking on the phone" but never of "listening on the phone." If two people are talking, the question of listening does not come up. It is almost as if we think of listening as being private, what goes on in the head, and talking is what is public. In pointing to a conversation, we point to that which is visible, that which is public. And because listening is thought of as a private and passive activity rather than a public one, we have not developed a science of listening. We have not thought about the nuances of how to listen. In our field, we have not asked, what is it to listen to an architect, or to listen to

Paul Rudolph, Art and Architecture Building, Yale University, New Haven, Connecticut, 1961–63.

a building? Architects are so busy talking that they forget to listen. They act as if they do not have time to listen to each other or to their clients. In fact, listening to your client is a polemical position. For architects to declare that they are very interested in the unique interests of their clients is already to take a particular position, like Neutra, presenting himself as an especially gifted listener and having himself photographed listening to his clients, blurring the role of the architect and the role of the shrink, the shrink being the paradigm of the listener. Most architects simply pretend they are not listening because it is a sign of strength not to listen, to be the one who talks. As architects get more and more successful, they stop going to conferences that they are not speaking at and spend less and less time listening to the other speakers. They stop listening, even to their own voices, perhaps.

Most architects talk past each other. In a sense, they are simply rivals competing for a part of the audience share. This audience, for example, has been carved up again and again by each successive speaker. But architects do listen in private. Privately they actually admit a lot of doubt. What is unique about the teaching of architecture in the university is the extent to which architects are able to tacitly admit that they do not really know what a building is. Even the buildings they inhabit every day. Do we really have the capacity to understand the effect of the ceiling above us here, for example? I am not so sure, despite the fact that most of us are architects and we have been in this room now for a long time. There is an enormous difference between the way architects operate in private, that is, in the studio, whether it be the studio of a school of architecture or the studio of an office, and how they behave in public, whether it be in a lecture, a conference, or a publication. The difference between the way we talk and listen in the studio and the way we talk and listen in conferences is much bigger than that between classical and avant-garde traditions. The line between the private side of the discourse and the public is the real line to discuss.

A quick example. When the first Royal Academy of Architecture was founded in the late seventeenth century, the whole point was that the leaders of the field, the select eight members of the academy, would go behind closed doors once a week to debate the fundamental issues, arguing about what the rules should really be, trying to establish agreement on what constitutes the language. When they made an agreement on a key issue, like whether the proportional module should be adjusted here or there, the conclusion would be presented publicly in lectures given by the director twice a week, starting with François Blondel in 1671. That is to say, doubt behind closed doors, although the members kept detailed private minutes of the disagreements, and then unambiguous public pronouncement. Very public. Anyone was welcome to walk in and listen. The lectures were certainly not compulsory for what were later understood to be architectural students. The young architects would go to hear the lectures simply to get some idea of what the jury would be thinking when they were judging the drawings submitted for the big competitions. In other words, students went looking for design clues. Eventually, the public lectures were turned into books and published as standard doctrines, starting with Blondel's *Cours* of 1675. The most confident statements circulated in the most public space. So we have a superconfident classical tradition in public, a tradition that even says that the classical is the very source of all confidence, which is actually filled with doubt behind closed doors.

In these terms, you could say that Paul Rudolph's Art and Architecture Building preserves the classical architecture of the discipline. What is put near the front door, if "front door" is a term you can still use with that building, is the exhibition space, library, and below, lecture theater. That is to say, there is a series of large public spaces in which the most confident statements of the discipline will be made. In a sense, the whole operation of the discipline is laid out between the café on the roof and the lecture hall in the basement, from the small space above, where everybody is eating, drinking, and talking at once, to the big room down below, where there is only one person standing in front with a clear message and everybody is respectfully quiet. Just below the café are the studios: massive disorder. This does not look anything at all like the Rudolph drawings of what was meant to go on there, with all his carefully drawn furniture neatly organized in the plans. What happens these days in the studios is that a kind of clearing is made in the middle of the wilderness for the pin-ups. It is usually a mess in the outer fringes of the space where the work is produced. This disorderly fringe ringing the volume is not just the space of production. It is also a space of reception, where teachers listen to students in a particular way. They sit side by side at the drawing desk, with one listening to the other and speaking lightly like a shrink: "So, what do you think you were doing with that column this week?" "Well, I don't know, but . . ." Eventually, enough confidence is built up in the evolving projects that the students can talk about their work in front of each other in the weekly pin-up. This is slightly more public, so a little bit of a clearing is made in the middle of the space, but all of the chairs of the class are usually gathered in a very tight defensive circle around the drawings and models as if it is understood that no one knows for sure what is going on and the outside world has to be kept at bay while the unformed shapes and ideas are nurtured. But something is already growing, gaining force. Eventually, the new life form becomes so strong, with a sufficiently strong story being told about it by the student, that it can be exposed a little more. So now the middle of the studio floor is really cleaned up and some teachers from other studios are invited in to see it and offer their reactions in a midterm review. Hopefully the work survives that assault, which involves a range of people with different philosophies throwing alternative descriptions at the project, seeing which words stick and which do not, and the student agilely adjusting to the rival narrative streams and learning how to talk. When the project and the story told about it finally mature, all disorder in the entire studio volume is cleared away and a group of outside experts comes in to judge it, the final jury. Big names from near and far. Now the lines of seats for the jury, class, and visitors are exactly parallel, the clear organization of the room matching the clear organization of the project and its narrative. The confident student is positioned in front of the firing line like a lecturer delivering a decisive presentation. Cameras and tape recorders appear to keep a public record. And if the project is really successful, it might then make its way down to the public exhibition space where anybody can come in off the street and see it. There is not so much talk in the display area, just a single set of images; the speaking voice of the designer is replaced with a few statements attached to the boards, as if the work now speaks for itself. And if it is one of the very best projects of the year, it will move out of the school as part of the official publicity. So the project gradually moves from doubt, mess, and multiple voices upstairs toward the front door and eventually out into the world as a clear singular statement.

And in that outside world, absolute confidence. Architects act as if any public admission of vulnerability or doubt will ruin a project. As if architecture, to be architecture, has to be certain. Even certain about uncertainty. Peter Eisenman may cultivate uncertainty relative to traditional norms but still must look society in the eye and say the impossible: "I know exactly how this project of mine is going to be uncertain. I am certain of that." And it is hard because deep down he loves architecture. He loves the fact that he has no fixed definitive idea of what the object is. Nor does Leon Krier, who must look the client in the eye and say, "I am certain that this is certain." There is surely a voice inside both saying, "perhaps . . . I am not sure . . . I wonder if . . . I hope . . ." What has happened at this conference today is that we have left the Art and Architecture Building behind, and crossed the street to an even bigger space, presumably to make even more confident statements. Which is why it was a pleasure to listen to Maurice express doubt, to see him place a remarkable image—the one of the car, the two doors open, the mother, the son, and the father presumably taking the photograph—alongside one of Rudolph as he asks, "Why? Why was I copying Rudolph? I do not know." The discipline works hard to resist such admissions of doubt. It literally structures itself to keep doubt private. If you look closely at Rudolph's original drawings for the A&A Building, for example, the jury space on the upper levels is in a semicircle, individual seats organized in a tight defensive formation, while the jury space that he draws inside the exhibition space below has all the seats absolutely in parallel, as if there is a sense that the discourse, when it is able to go down into the public world, is lined up, open, has nothing to hide.

And here we are, lined up in our teams, confident, expressing with great certainty what we believe, who we like and do not like. This event is supposedly all about making conflict public, bringing a big fight from the private meetings of Leon and Peter into the public sphere. But this is a conflict that has always been staged in public. In private, there is absolutely no evidence of conflict between these two figures—intellectual, emotional, physical, or otherwise. This is because it is not really a conflict. The positions are so symmetrical that there is no dissonance or exchange. Each side, in fact, adjusts to become the opposite of the other. It is funny reading the 1983 *Skyline* interview. Peter is desperately trying to seek agreement, and he keeps saying, "I think you will agree that . . ." and every time Leon is very careful to not agree. There is no agreement at all, no real discussion, just a kind of simultaneous intergalactic missile launch: all the weapons launched by the protagonists pass each other overhead, hitting people in the back of the room but leaving the two of them intact, superintact, given the flames that now rise up in the distance. In fact, it seems that they use each other in public to finely tune their positions: "If Leon is going that way, I should have gone that way." It is enormously useful to find out who you are by looking at somebody who is meant to be what you are not. It's so relentlessly symmetrical in the end that it is actually a single position. So tight, so organic, so ecologically balanced and sustainable is this relationship that it is a single position. Which is why, I suppose, the catalog for the exhibition here at Yale puts one-half of each of their heads together to form one combined head. It is inconceivable that one of the sides, left brain or right, will today hear something in the other that changes it. They will not really listen to each other; they cannot listen and preserve their radicality. And yet, if they are typical architects, they will listen to each other in private. The doubt will yet again be behind closed doors. On April 8, 2002, in Milan, Peter Eisenman was asked by an interviewer, "Do you discuss your work with other architects?" And he answered immediately, "Yes, all the time. Like Leon Krier; today we had lunch." And this is how it goes, the public statement of an affectionate meeting in private. He moves on to say that he also enjoys having lunch with Rafael Moneo, Philip Johnson, Jeff Kipnis, Mark Wigley, and Robert Stern before repeating the point that he really disagrees with Leon Krier, but respects him a lot. When asked, "Where do you work on your designs and projects?" he says, "I have a studio. My office is like an atelier and I have a desk in there. I do not have my own office. I sit in the middle of my studio. We have about 20 or 30 people, and I am able to listen to what is going on. I have no private telephone. It is where I do all my work, my drawing, my thinking." This is a classic image of the architect's studio as a laboratory, in which architecture is somehow mystically created, with a listening post at its center. The architect's images of certainty, the precise drawings and clear public statements, are created out of a confrontation with doubt. Anyway, it is only when facing doubt that you are forced to make a decision. It is only when there is no clear rationale that will tell you what the next move is that you must make a decision, that you must draw a line, must act as an architect. So it is not a surprise that architects secretly cherish doubt. Doubt is, as it were, the beginning of architecture. Unsure, the architect listens. Leon Krier is even wary of people who sit in the middle of their studio and listen too much. When he negotiates his separation from a once close relationship with Jim Stirling, he writes his open letter of 1976, in which he complains that Stirling did not admit to the effect Krier had on his designs when he worked in his studio, and indeed went so far as to remove Krier's name from the credits of projects. In 1976, a year before Peter and Leon came out as a couple, we have this statement from Krier about Stirling: "I have never, in fact, met a professional who could like you be a patient listener, who could accept ideas and suggestions so candidly. You seem in certain cases to appropriate some of these strange collective design objects only as they merge into the public realm." He is not complaining that Stirling did not listen, which is what every generation accuses the other generation of—the young saying that the old don't listen and the old saying that the young don't listen. Rather, the accusation is that the older generation listened too closely, absorbing and claiming what was said.

But such a literal absorption of what the other says is not listening. To listen is not just to hear and repeat somebody's words. To listen is to be open, to obey what is said, not who seems to be saying it. To listen is to take the risk of being deeply affected in ways you cannot predict. This does not mean that you obey the explicit letter of what you hear. Listening is never the simple absorption of a message. It is the way of opening yourself to the unknown, welcoming whatever lurks within whatever you hear, welcoming, as it were, whatever stranger might walk in. It includes listening, by the way, to interruptions, like those of today. It is not passive. It is highly active. To listen is to be faithful to what you hear, but in order to be really faithful you have to invent new norms, new ways of listening, new contexts for what you hear, in the very name of what you hear. To listen carefully is to hear what the person who is talking cannot hear in what they are saying. And there cannot be any outside authority for these new norms, no way to legitimate these new ways of listening. Good listeners always rearrange what they hear. Listening, I am suggesting, is an art, an art that can be taught. In my opinion, architectural studios are an extraordinary model of this teaching. Without ever discussing it, we teach our students how to listen. And yet it is disappointing that this special form of listening always gives way to an overconfident rhetoric in public, this kind of generic arrogance of the architect, the strutting confidence about that thing we secretly know and love simply for the fact that we have never figured out really what it is. The risky art of listening unfortunately gives way to the safety of loud speeches. Perhaps the rise of so-called theory in architecture in the last fifteen years, this rise that people like Roger Kimball pretend to be so upset about—surely one could not really be so upset about what architects are talking about today, since they have an absolutely minimal impact on the cultural and political world—is simply the fact that the doubt has perhaps been taken from behind the closed doors and made somewhat public. So-called theory in architecture, I would suggest, is simply listening. It is not taking a singular position. It is not a call to arms. Nothing ever comes directly out of it. On the contrary, it is a deepening and widening of the possibilities at any one moment. It is simply a form of research that puts the doubt that permeates the studio world into the lecture hall and the exhibition space. The unembarrassed display of doubt acts as an invitation, even a demand, for people to take responsibility for their next move, calling for thoughtful gestures without specifying them. Making public this doubt is utterly in the spirit of a university like this one, and utterly in the spirit of our love of architecture.

Architects, to conclude, are obsessed with the intimate play between certainty and uncertainty. All of us know that the objects we and our students produce act for our society as the very image of certainty. And yet we also know that we do not really know what these objects are, how we produce them, or how they will be experienced. We have plenty of theories, plenty of what was yesterday called opinions—when, remarkably, Alberti was described as somebody who just had opinions. Nevertheless, it is precisely there, in this obsession with the play between certainty and uncertainty, that our irrational love of architecture lies. This is just simply to say that what we love about architecture is precisely that it forever blurs and defeats the line drawn right down through the middle of this conference. That is to say, the line between certainty and uncertainty, comfort and anxiety, the line that supposedly divides our happy couple but actually binds them together forever and forever.

THE

ARCHITECTS

The Arcadian, the Utopian, and Junkspace

Peter Eisenman

As Colin Rowe was fond of quoting, "Facts are like sacks; if you don't fill them with values, they won't stand up." The question of values is important in any discussion framed as two ideologies, particularly since values are at the root of ideology. Any discussion of values includes a light side and a dark side. Privately, I have always thought that I am the white knight to Leon Krier's black knight. But anyone, including myself, who makes such distinctions has to be careful, and no one is more careful in such instances than Mark Wigley. He knows that there is always a hidden agenda behind such black-and-white divisions, which are set up to ensnare anyone who believes that such an arrangement is innocent of other agendas. Indeed, it is precisely these other, perhaps unspoken, agendas that in their absence dominate the thematic of this conference.

The title of my talk, "The Arcadian, the Utopian, and Junkspace," reflects an idea that operating in architecture today there are not two but at least three differing ideologies with respect to the city. One is the arcadian, represented here by Leon Krier. This worldview implies a return to some notion of a lost paradise, of a simpler, more accessible time. In one sense, it is an attempt to stop the forward motion of time, to suggest that there is an architectural language that is stable and known, that the scale of the Greek orders and their symbolic meaning are still valid today. It is underpinned by an idea that people and their social organizations, represented in their desires for place, have changed very little. This is argued in the current American ideal, that is, the American suburb, in the principle that underlies the misnomer

New Urbanism, advocated by Andrés Duany and Elizabeth Plater-Zyberk, and in the various classicisms proposed by Krier, Porphyrios, Culot, and others. But people have changed since the time of ancient Greece, if not physically, then psychologically; their mobility has also changed.

The utopian, which I represent at this conference, reflects a continuing desire for an unattainable better future. This idea of social progress fueled modernism's program of community. Clearly, modernism, and with it the radical political ideology of the left, failed not only intellectually and socially but also architecturally. Its idea of the good society was capital's idea of the good life. Nevertheless, the impetus for change is still present, although today the question must be, in what context?

The third ideology, not represented at this conference, can be characterized by Rem Koolhaas's so-called junkspace. Like Georges Bataille's attack on architecture, it is not so much an ideology as it is a facile critique of the detritus of modernism and the modernist utopia. It denies not only Krier's arcadian dream but also just about every other kind of project, including those of Koolhaas's very corporate clients, who regard his chic criticism of a bored elite as just another bit of fun. But Koolhaas is serious. His project is the very denial of all projects. Junkspace is like a nihilism fulfilled, where place has become so detached from dwelling that we find ourselves, as Massimo Cacciari says, in an absurd labyrinth. Junkspace describes a condition that, without a prescription for amelioration, only allows matters to continue to worsen. In the face of such unrelenting cynicism, Koolhaas is portraying, like Robert Musil's *The Man Without Qualities*—who possesses so many qualities that he is unable to choose—the architectural equivalent—a world without qualities. Like Sartre's *No Exit* or Camus's *The Stranger*, it leaves one in the suffocation of a void, not a void of nothingness but a void filled with the detritus of modernism.

According to Cacciari, the negative project that is so much a part of modernism is no longer useful when it achieves its goal, that is, when it becomes nihilistic. Koolhaas's attempt to charge universal uprootedness in the form of junkspace with qualities creates an impotent pathos of nostalgia. To combine the equivalent of exchange with the pretended authenticity of use, Cacciari contends, is not a project.

One of the major differences between the three ideologies is the status of the negative. In the arcadian project, the negative is hardly a factor. In the utopian/modernist project, it plays an animating role, while in junkspace it has become nihilistic.

Ultimately, the negative only operates as a project in a critical, as opposed to a cynical, context. Cacciari would characterize the rift between a Koolhaas and a Krier as being between the metropolitan project as a project of negativity and as the symbolic, religious, and cultural rootedness of dwelling. But the idea of the metropolitan in the OMA name cannot be overlooked: it concerns the liberation of the idea of space from place. From the Heideggerian notion of being and its phenomenology, the metropolitan is a rootless urban nomad existing in abstract mathematical (and perhaps now algebraic) space. This is opposed to both the city and country dwellers who are organized around a ground and, more important, a center—which is viewed as static as well as mobile.

The idea of the negative not as dialectical but as enfolded within any condition of the positive deals with the issue of the present and, ultimately, with presence and the present of presence. If the becoming unmotivated of the metaphysics of presence—that is, the removal of traditional codes, conventions, and continuities—can be considered a dominant problem today, and if abstraction can be seen to have failed in this respect, then perhaps an enfolded negative, one that internally erodes the fullness of presence (that is, its metaphysic) is a possibility.

It is this possibility that defines a difference in the critique of the present offered by the arcadian and utopian projects. The arcadian attempts to re-create a version of a past language in the future; the utopian offers a critique that attempts to transform or displace language itself to create a new or different future. While the utopian and the abstract impulses of modernism may have failed, the notion of modernism as a generic sociopolitical critique that began in the late eighteenth century is still with us. It merely takes other forms today. The shift from the analogic to the digital is one of these.

Both modernist and junkspace ideologies are critiques of the metaphysical project, in particular, the metaphysics of presence, but here the similarity ends. Equally, to characterize my project as one of a failed utopia is an ironic gesture for the purposes of this conference, because the gaps between my project and the modernist utopia of abstraction are large. Ultimately, my project is defined by the following: the arbitrariness of the linguistic relationship of sign to signified; the negation of the conventions of metaphysics, which sustain the bourgeois idea of presence; and ideas of space versus place. These critiques ultimately separate Krier and Koolhaas from my project. In the end, these critiques attempt to overcome the passivity of the spectacle in favor of a more active cognitive relationship between building and viewer. These displacements offer the possibility of incorporating a negativity that brings the passion of the Dionysian into contact with both the arcadian and the abstract without requiring a synthesis.

Coming to Terms with Janus

Leon Krier

Peter did well to stay away from the symposium's opening massacre by Roger Kimball. It is a bone-chilling experience to have to witness politely one's own public execution. The auditorium's nervous chuckles following the terminator's bloody strikes were, I hoped against hope, caused by the relief of not having their own heads on the block and not by the spectacle of my crucifixion. What can Peter's and my own work possibly have in common to attract a unilateral nemesis? In politically more excitable situations, such inquisitorial finger-pointing leads irreversibly to public lynching. Mr. Kimball's cold fury reminded me of Ellsworth Toohey's contained jealous rages. I cannot understand it any better than his awkward pronunciation of French words.

The gods be thanked, for Yale is neither his turf nor his occasion or public. Also, Dean Stern is to be thanked for having made this school into a true academy, where divergent political, aesthetic, and architectural doctrines are taught and debated in a climate of respect and tolerance. Whether we are able to honor the challenge is an open question. Intellectual bulldozing and moralistic brand marking are, I hope, not at home here. Scandalously few schools and institutions cultivate what is, after all, the spirit of democracy and inquiry. Peter's Institute for Architecture and Urban Studies did while it lasted, and Alvin Boyarsky's Architectural Association was its lone champion in the early 1970s. Like a spoiled kid, I considered it then a given to teach beside Peter Cook, Elia Zenghelis, and Bernard Tschumi. I found it quite normal to be invited regularly to the IAUS and for Peter to send us to tour thirteen universities around the United States. That is how I met Andrés Duany, Elizabeth Plater-Zyberk, Jaquelin Robertson, the people who most changed my life. I am now fully aware of the privilege it is to be at Yale, for the ideological shutters came down in the mid-1980s. As a consequence, most architecture schools in the democratic countries are quite unable to hold a symposium such as this. I only began to appreciate fully the meaning of democracy to me personally when, as the result of my book on Albert Speer, I was branded. Even though I was not physically persecuted or arrested, for a while I lost the fighting chance I had so foolishly taken for granted.

Maurice Culot's touching performance today and his reluctance to grab the Speer problem by the neck can be better understood in the light of what we both had to go through after publishing the book. What we wanted to reassess, and what many people still refuse to discuss even now, was not Speer's guilt but the question of whether a monstrous criminal can be a great architect and, conversely, whether a great architect's moral guilt necessarily reduces the quality of his architecture. It is generally accepted that a pathological criminal can be a great general, scientist, engineer, industrialist, musician; why not a great architect? All criminal totalitarian regimes of the twentieth century have used classical and modernist architecture equally for their perverse political purposes. Why should classical architecture be found guilty by that association when modernism, industrial technology, and design, communications, and armament systems are at the same time held to be morally neutral and therefore available for unrestricted use and development?

The cold arrogance, imperial ruthlessness, and repressiveness of some of Speer's buildings lay not, we thought, in their classical style but in their size, scale, and ideological program. Whether Speer, Le Corbusier, or Mies van der Rohe designed Hitler's parade grounds, party monuments, and death camps would not change the fundamental criminality of their social and political purpose. Indeed, many modernist projects and realizations are arguably more totalitarian than Speer's visions. Ludwig Hilberseimer turned the whole of Friedrichstrasse into an architectural gulag. If a criminal architect does not necessarily design criminal buildings, an innocuous mind does not in turn automatically produce innocent architecture.

The scale comparisons we published demonstrated that the size and scale of Nazi urbanism and architecture were perfectly in tune with those of any other contemporary industrial regime, whether democratic or totalitarian. The scaleless brutality of the Plan Voisin, of Brasilia, of metabolist utopias, even of Manhattan zoning, by far exceeded that of Speer's vainest schemes. The reprehensible side of Nazi architecture, we demonstrated, is not its classical and traditional aspects but its radical collectivism and technological modernism, its hubris of limitless expansion and progress. It is the global triumph of exactly these values that, notwithstanding the destruction of Nazism and communism, condemns the very existence of humankind on this

Leon Krier, portrait of Peter Eisenman, 1977.

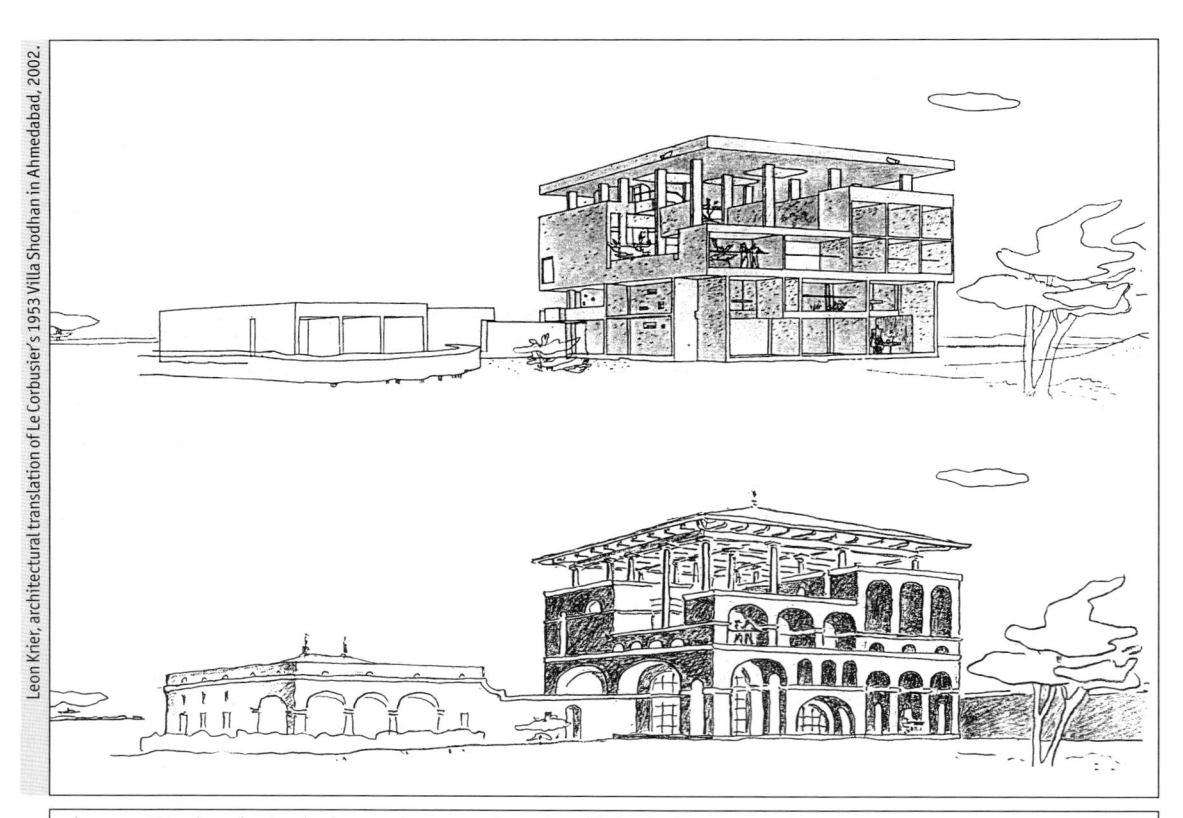

Leon Krier, architectural translation of Le Corbusier's 1953 Villa Shodhan in Ahmedabad, 2002.

planet. Waxing lyrical about the moral and political virginity of modernism is quite simply farcical. A one-hour walk around New Haven and what little survived the modernist rape, maybe a similar circular look from the top floor of our hotel, should suffice to open our Candide's eyes and bury forever their angelicism. Mr. Kimball instead correctly understood that both Peter's and my work is born out of a radical criticism of modernism. Instead of our rejection or deconstruction of it, he would have preferred us to behave like good boys and try something down Louis Kahn's way.

Of course, if you must stay within modernism's narrow waveband, Kahn isn't such a bad register; but who exactly says you must? Between the ages of sixteen and twenty-four, I strictly followed that imperative and forced myself to forget that the big wide world of architecture and urbanism offered far more satisfying choices. After all, I had grown up in an environment that, despite two recent world wars, was unblemished by modernist architecture and planning until the mid-1960s. Luxembourg was a jewel of traditional architecture, a small capital city embedded in a manicured landscape and lofty beech forests. I had most of my secondary education in a baroque abbey in the small medieval town of Echternach, which together with its four-tower Romanesque basilica, had in less than ten years been beautifully reconstructed in a fully artisan way after near total destruction during the 1944 Rundstedt offensive. During our holidays, my family traveled to France, Switzerland, and Italy, not to study "dead history" but to admire beautiful living towns and landscapes. Like Luxembourg, they were mostly untouched by modernism. When at long last I got to take my parents to visit something modern, Le Corbusier's Marseille block left us all speechless with shock. Not one of us, not even I myself, could believe that this was what I had been admiring in pictures and texts for so long. For weeks I tried to overcome my unavoidable disappointment. I found myself for the first time in my life justifying to my parents something I deeply felt to be unacceptable.

The relentless modernist degradation of Luxembourg, which started in earnest a few years later, alienated me not only from my cherished birthplace but, more radically, from modernism, the intellectual homeland in which I had sought temporary refuge from what I erroneously thought to have been a mere provincial upbringing. What I had learned at university and in Jim Stirling's office about the possibilities of modernist architecture was clearly inferior to the architectural environment I had grown up in. Even the best of the Corbusier, Terragni, and Mies that I by then had visited nowhere fulfilled the bloated promises of their pamphlets. Both the formal and technological aspects of the artisan reconstruction of a Luxembourg village that I had witnessed in my youth outdid in speed and quality those aspects of modernist propaganda.

So what was it all about? What was the historical cataclysm beyond which there was no possible return and which was so blatantly denied by my own experience? For me and most of the people I deal with every day, traditional architecture and urbanism are not, and never were, a dead thing of the past. They are part of our lives in the same way our languages are. Now I ask you, what if a sect came along with a fabricated "newspeak" and claimed it to be the only truly modern language? They would form an influential lobby infiltrating all systems of education and communications, imposing the view that all traditional classical languages—French, Chinese, English, Russian, Bantu—were historical and dated, and therefore anyone who spoke them was a historicist, a nostalgic, a reactionary, or worse. World architecture has been suffering this kind of nightmare scenario for four generations, and as a result, 95 percent of the globe's vernacular and classical architecture has been wiped out or degraded. The diseases that devastated indigenous populations as a result of European colonization offer a striking parallel to modernism's lethal effect.

Neither Roger Kimball nor neomodernists seem preoccupied by that cultural holocaust. They busy themselves instead with reiterating legitimizations for what happened. In my opinion, modernism has not (yet) produced an architecture and building technology that can be compared in quality and versatility to any of the identifiable traditional classical and vernacular cultures. It is merely a vernacular of concrete, steel, and glass that has not matured into a viable architectural

Leon Krier, "Transformation of 1965 Tower Block. Piazza Marconi Alessandria (I)," 1998–2002.

TRANSFORMATION of 1965 Tower Block Piazza

Marconi Alessandria (I)   Leon KRIER 1998-2002

and urban language, that is, one that is apt to replace in time all buildings and settlement patterns around the world, regardless of climate, geography, and culture. I have no doubt that out of modernism's manyfold heritages an architectural language could be developed in the same way that an authoritarian imposition of Esperanto would eventually produce a literature, a poetry, and a rhetoric. The latter, however, could never replace the wealth of the classical languages and the vernacular. So what can possibly be the significance of architectural deconstruction? Despite its forced intellectual and weak practical premises, it occupies a lot of space in the media, in public commissions, and ultimately in academia. I personally enjoy some of its products and welcome it as the final phase of modernism's corrosion. There is, however, a meaning to deconstruction of which few of its proponents are aware: it is a cry in the darkness, a protest with confused motivations, and yet, like any daft theory or religion, it may produce in the hands of gifted designers like Peter, Frank Gehry, or Zaha Hadid interesting plastic and moving artistic results. Nevertheless, to propose deconstruction as a general theory for urbanism and architecture is in my opinion unsustainable; to build entire villages, cities, landscapes, and countries, or systematically intervene in traditionally formed environmental contexts according to deconstructivism's arcana, would be absurd, if it weren't impractical and unaffordable.

In linguistics, deconstruction and decryption are established means of evidencing the constitutive elements of a text or a word, of laying bare its evident and hidden meanings or structures. Their ultimate goal is reconstruction and information, not confusion or revolt. What has become known as architectural deconstruction is an entirely different affair. It represents a state of crisis of architectural modernism. It occupies itself not with the deconstruction but rather with the destruction, destructuring, fragmenting of modernist building types, elements, aesthetics. It does not put into question, dialogue with, or replace the theory and practice of traditional architecture. That is quite simply not its concern. The buildings of Eisenman, Gehry, and Hadid are gut reactions against the scalelessness and collectivism, the oppressive massiveness, the cloned repetitiveness, and ultimately against the obsolete industrial imperatives of modernism.

Paradoxically, what can be mistaken for expressions of violence and grief often turn out to have the contrary effect. Deconstructivism's practice of breaking up large building programs into a multiplicity of smaller fragments makes its buildings more approachable than the bland, scaleless faceless bulks of routine modernism. The latter's mind-killing uniformity and semantic emptiness the literal embodiments of a totalitarianism that destroys individuality, family, society—indeed life—are turned here into picturesque ruins. Didn't the shattered remnants of the World Trade Center look shockingly as if Frank Gehry had designed them? They were not ruins of architecture but ruins of modernism. How can this lead to anything more than the celebration of protest, chaos, or tragedy, and hence of crisis, in the literal meaning of transition?

Peter's urban scheme for Berlin, the Klingelhöfer-Dreieck Housing of 1991–93, looked in plan remarkably like the old hill town in which I presently live. You cannot find in either one a single truly straight line or right angle. The buildings twist and bend like organic bodies; they lean over backward and forward and never describe abstract, pure, Euclidean figures. They neither bore nor overwhelm. They look natural but actually are not.

When approaching Gehry's Guggenheim Bilbao, I was reminded more of piled rock formations or drifting icebergs than of anything architectural—whether modernist or traditional. The "train crash," "ruins," "shards," and "earthquake" metaphors so often associated with such buildings are not accidental. These appellations, however, do not so much reveal the essence of the objects as deride their intentions. Natural mineral landscapes are always eroded, broken up, or ruined versions of previously differently shaped and constituted solids. They are as far removed from the abstractions of modernism as they are from the geometric figures and typological inventions of traditional architecture and urbanism. I believe that despite its declared ambitions of creating a new architecture, deconstructivism represents but an escape from modernism, the tyranny of excessive abstraction giving way to the yearning for an impossible "naturalness."

Traditional architecture instead is a complete man-made artifice. It does not imitate natural organic or mineral forms but has its own artificial elements: the wall, the window, the door, the roof, the column, the architrave, the arch, carpentry, and so on. It is technological and tectonic and, like organic nature, typological, reproductive, and adaptive. Traditional architecture creates an inventory of building types, elements, techniques, and settlement patterns for which there are no direct precedents, only metaphors in nature. As Hannah Arendt pointed out, that very artificiality makes it into a properly human and humane invention.

AFTERWORD

Vincent Scully

It's wonderful after a long day of talking to hear the two aging lions roar at last, these scarred veterans of the critical and the building wars. Still, closing remarks are difficult to make. In this case I have felt that Alan Plattus should be making them, since his introduction to this event, published in *Constructs*, is a masterful analysis of the relationship of these two architects to each other. It's also hard to wait around all day fearing that everything worth saying will be said by somebody else.

Occasionally, too, one feels required to respond to an earlier talk, perhaps negatively. I find that painful, as it is for me in saying a word about Roger Kimball's provocative—indeed, considering the circumstances, spunky—keynote address. I must say at once that I do not concur in the intemperate characterization of it that we heard earlier this afternoon. But it was calculated to provoke a response, and it certainly provoked me. It was highly destructive of everybody except Geoffrey Scott —especially, appropriately enough, Leon and Peter. I suppose that it is the right, even the duty, of a critic to denounce what he doesn't like, or thinks is destructive of the public weal. But Mr. Kimball's talk upset me badly, not because of its familiar ideas but because it seemed so unloving, so uncharitable, in tone. Perhaps I am wrong, and no one else was bothered by that, but I couldn't help thinking of 1 Corinthians: "Though I speak with the tongues of men and of angels, and have not charity, I am become as sounding brass, or a tinkling cymbal."

In this case what was suggested was less cymbals than a tight little snare drum rattling files of convicts to the chair. Corinthians goes on: "Charity suffereth long, and is kind; charity envieth not; charity vaunteth not itself, is not puffed up . . . seeketh not her own."

Good advice for all of us, not only Mr. Kimball. But what is most interesting in this connection is that charity involves a feeling for others (vaunteth not itself); there is in it a sense of identification with persons and things outside the self. And in this, it resembles the late-nineteenth- and early-twentieth-century psychological concept of empathy, which may be roughly defined as the physical identification of the viewer with the object viewed. That concept was fairly pervasive in the architectural criticism of the period: in Eidlitz, Sullivan, Worringer very specifically in 1910, and most to the point, Geoffrey Scott in 1914. You will remember that Scott set up a number of what he called "fallacies," fallacious ways of approaching architecture: the romantic fallacy, the mechanical, the ethical, the biological. He discards them all in favor of "humanist values," which are founded on empathy, on the physical identification of the human being with the building. There are some beautiful descriptions of the body sensing, the mind embracing, tracing the swell of the vault and the dome. Scott writes, "The eye and the mind must travel together; thought and vision move at one pace and in step." That's pretty good, I think. Empathy may be passé for critics who practice lit crit, but it's still useful to me.

Perhaps that's a disadvantage today. Empathy, charity, love: love unmans us and unfits us for destructive criticism and, pitifully I suppose, leaves us able to write only about what we like. The great Henri Focillon advised his students to do just that. Perhaps all critics should discipline themselves in that way for a while. It is sad to feel, however unjustly, that a critic has never loved a building, and I'm afraid that applies not only to Mr. Kimball.

Anyway, like Mr. Kimball, and most of the rest of us here, I suspect, I have been dragooned into these remarks by a dominant personality, my friend Dean Robert Stern. And I have had serious reservations about them. It seemed to me at first that today's event arose out of a contrived and artificial program and so suggested an artificial and contrived response, and that bothered me. Nor did Dean Stern mention this Nolli-Piranesi business to me, perhaps to spare my blood pressure, since Yale has recently been ridiculed in the popular press by a not so popular critic for being, according to him, obsessed with Nolli, while we all knew it was Cornell.

The real heart of the problem is the Krier-Eisenman comparison. Surely the conjunction of Leon and Peter, two major heavyweights who are here at Yale this term, may be taken as the latest result of Dean Stern's abiding determination to induce the lion and the lamb to lie down together—though one would think that neither of these gentlemen could ever qualify for the latter category. Yet they have both become such kind and understanding old duffers in these, their riper years, and are so obviously fond of each other, that they come across as fairly lamblike after all. Still, the intention was clearly to bring together two totally different architectural personalities and ideologies and to see what happened: mayhem or, as I'm sure Dean Stern believed, the discovery of some common ground between them. Or perhaps the intention was simply to show that opposing views of architecture can coexist without the world ending, Yale's famous pluralism triumphant once more.

That last is easy to affirm, perhaps all too easy: to declare a happy concordance between the two champions, a sacred truce covering all. There are certainly many sympathetic similarities to recommend both of them to us. They are compulsive teachers. That touches us where we live. In fact, they were teaching before they were building, and they first built in order to teach. They work at teaching; they do their homework. They care about subject and students alike, and their teaching and example have changed the architectural landscape in several important if fundamentally different ways. As teachers, though, they are alike in the fact that their verbal language bears a direct relationship to their architectural language. Not that they, especially Peter, necessarily mean what they say all the time, but the structure of their language is like that of their architecture: classically laconic and incisive in Leon's, densely interwoven and allusive—even elusive—in Peter's. Today, though, they seem to have borrowed each other's style: Peter clear and incisive, Leon ruminative and discursive. Still, their sentences normally do suggest their forms. And what can be more important than that for teachers of a formal language when, like Freud's dreamwork, it has to be described and analyzed in words?

So Peter and Leon convince both us and their students that their words are not smoke screens behind which their true intentions lurk, as was normally the case in my youth, when the chanting of threadbare slogans—"form follows function," "space-time," "organic architecture," or simply "our time"—generally took the place of thought. Indeed, only one restrictive way of thinking and acting was allowed in those years. There was a deeply totalitarian mindset in modern architecture in the decades directly after World War II. That is why people of my age tend to be wary of architectural theory, especially of ideologies professed by architects to explain or enhance their own work. (I have, unhappily, heard one or two slogans chanted today.) It is different with Leon and Peter, but I do believe that in this newly intrinsic interaction between language, architecture, and thought that began in the 1960s, Robert Venturi's *Complexity and Contradiction* (1966) first opened the way. Venturi was obviously thinking afresh in forms and words and dared to say things outside the International Style canon of discourse; and the chanters of slogans hated him for it, feared him for it. He was writing empathically about architectural form; later he and Denise Scott Brown were to explore the related and long-neglected issue of architectural sign and symbol in *Learning from Las Vegas* (1972) and in their buildings. Here I do not mean to belittle Colin Rowe's important critical and pedagogical achievements of the 1960s, but since they were not properly published at the time, only his students could know much about them, not the rest of us in the far-off world beyond. Consequently, Venturi bore the brunt of the profession's savage reaction to this assault on its sullen anti-intellectualism, an assault that Eisenman and Krier were soon to take up and sustain, each in his own fashion. *Five Architects*, for example, was written more or less in response to Venturi's book; it is hard to imagine the second without the first. Even more to the point, Eisenman miraculously brought the Institute for Architecture and Urban Studies into being, and it instantly became the center of the new discourse, its forum, a private institution of advanced education and debate, unique, I think, in contemporary architectural culture. It was all due to Peter, with some important opposition by Stern, and none of us, of whatever critical persuasion, can ever thank him (or them) enough for it. Therefore I have to disagree a little bit with my dear old friend and colleague Kurt Forster, so generous of spirit, whose words have so appropriately celebrated Peter's career: it was Venturi who cut the Gordian knot of modern architecture and theory, not Peter. Peter then tied a new one, much more intricate than the old, with many more strands (he tied many more strands together in his talk today than anyone else) involving several categories of ideas and encouraging architects and scholars of every shade of opinion, including Leon in those days, to do their work and have their say and pick at the knot for themselves.

It is true that both Peter and Leon have always had strong reservations about Venturi's ideas, but Peter's essential literary references, if not his full linguistic analogy, were already there in *Complexity and Contradiction*, as was Leon's respect for the solid lessons to be learned from architecture's classical and vernacular traditions and his willingness to employ their forms. Here Aldo Rossi should also be gratefully remembered. It's been all Tafuri today, never Rossi: another example among several at this conference of feeding by choice off criticism, not off architecture. Rossi must be cited here in relation to Leon for his perception in *Architettura della città* (also 1966) that architecture is not the individual masterpiece but the city as a whole—in other words, that architecture is not a collection of abstract works of art but a community of constructed buildings, wherein type and context are more significant than formal invention and individual style. Rossi went on to embody all of those fundamental ideas in his own luminous, haunting works.

Despite these similarities and whatever is common in their backgrounds, it is obvious that Leon and Peter are utterly different from one another in basic ways. Eisenman's method in his Houses I, II, and so on was indeed a revolutionary one. He really did deconstruct architecture and put it together again in a way that seemed to be purposely fragmented. He turned it inside out, and he tried to do the same with language, like his French friends. But he soon added a strong jolt of Russian so-called constructivism to the mixture, focusing on its explosive diagonals as Venturi had on its supergraphics and Suprematist color: a striking instance of the many times an incomplete historical experience has been taken up and developed by a later generation. And Peter's part in it did literally initiate the architectural deconstructivism of the present day.

Krier, on the other hand, and considering the climate of the time, did an even more revolutionary thing. He said, without equivocation and in the teeth of modernism's most sacred dogma, "We must rebuild the classical and vernacular traditions of architecture." Moreover, he insisted that those traditions were embodied in the traditional European city, which we had to rebuild as well. Nobody, not Venturi, not Rossi, had ever been so categorically intransigent, so uncompromising. Krier literally thought the unthinkable, said the unsayable. His remarkably powerful take on the European city in his projects for Parc de la Villette in Paris, *Roma Interrotta*, and so on, produced a much more convincing and three-dimensional urbanism than the flat *pochés* suggested to other architects by the Nolli plan (of which we have heard so much), which could not be brought satisfactorily into three dimensions using the prevailing Corbusian architectural vocabulary. Some of the architects involved eventually came to realize that traditional urbanism required more solid, more typical, probably more traditional architectural forms. Krier had known it from the beginning. Out of his example and tutelage, as Andrés Duany and Elizabeth Plater-Zyberk are the first to acknowledge, came, in large part, the New Urbanism of today—again, like Peter's deconstructivism, applauded by some and loathed by others. In contrast to the Koolhaas-Venturi and Eisenman-Krier *rapprochements* that have been cited today, New Urbanism has not been mentioned at all, not once. Does this suggest that it is the single element that is still too challenging, too modern, to be received into the new Grand Alliance? I applaud it, not only for funky, quirky Seaside, which is not at all the nostalgic village that its detractors want to believe it to be, but even more for HUD's Hope VI center-city projects, funded by the great Henry Cisneros. Hope VI exemplifies New Urbanist principles and represents the first time since modernism took over in the United States that architecture has done anything at all good for the poor, especially in the essential program of large-scale public housing. Charity? Only in the biblical sense. We need only walk straight up York and Ashmun Streets in New Haven to see what amounts to a paradise in comparison to the hellish no-man's-land of low-rise barracks and high-rise slabs that was there before. One can have no patience with architects or critics who deprecate that achievement (or with a federal administration that is trying to kill it).

The opposing, or contrasting, attitudes that Krier and Eisenman have championed over the years obviously have bitterly divided the profession. That split has become profoundly unpleasant. It has engendered the kind of sloganeering and nastiness we thought we had left behind in the 1960s. The major protagonists may like and respect each other, but most of their followers do not. Can all that be healed beyond a simple tolerance of each side for the other? Can we learn from one another, or is that, as Mark Wigley suggests, utterly inconceivable? Can Krier's and Eisenman's architectures be regarded as at all alike or as more or less equally useful to us in different ways, so fulfilling Dean Stern's sweetest dreams of peace?

Well, perhaps so, to a degree. At least, Peter and Leon both write about the physical experience of architecture, as not all of Peter's distant followers always do, and their buildings are physically powerful and aggressive in similar ways. Peter's celebrate kinetic energy: the dynamism, the danger in things. When one of the rogue beams of the Wexner Center comes slamming diagonally across space, following some weird trajectory in Peter's brain, and quivers to an unsupported stop just a foot or so away from a shuddering *pan de verre*, then we know that we have left behind, for example, the stable world of Louis I. Kahn. The Vitruvian man of perfect proportions no longer stands with his arms and legs extended in the center of the perfect humanist space of square and circle; he no longer holds the brute forces of matter apart with his inviolate presence. I suppose that's what Eisenman means when he refers to the "antihumanism" of his work. The heroic figure disappears. The forces fall in upon us: they pursue their intersecting ways according to complex laws outside ourselves. Peter usually convinces us somehow that they are real forces, ecological, contextual, geomantic, or mystical, just as his wholly hypothetical Mercator grid under Berlin tends to assure us that his building's intersecting stripes really have to be there. Like some of Malevich's titles, Peter's words supply an associational element to encourage our empathetic response to his forms. We are putty in his hands. He can be kind to us. He can make us laugh. He sends the facade of his Greater Columbus Convention Center rocking and rolling down the street, flopping along like a Newfoundland puppy, and making us wish for a moment that all streets were like that, though we know we'd soon be dizzy if they were. Then he does the same thing inside the building, bringing what ought to be long and dreary interior spaces into a wonderfully goofy, autonomous life.

Krier is exactly the opposite. He rebuilds classical humanism and its ideal stability, embraces the whole humanist tradition. Especially in his early writings, illustrated with overwhelming drawings, he loves a primitive humanism: a classicism at its beginnings, still in touch with animism, with barbarism. His buildings are easily as physical as Peter's, but they are utterly still, immanent, even ominous. Rita Wolff's wonderful paintings of them enhanced their magical qualities in those early days. They are somber. This is a classicism that broods, is tragic. There is melancholy in it and a physical longing for places. The barbarians are just off the page, perhaps in ourselves. We are founding a colony across the Rhine, in the shadow of the forest, or on the Danube, beyond which the Tartar steppe stretches to the eastern horizon. Those rustic capitals of wood—many of them to be built later at Seaside—those high, sharp gables, are there because Krier's is a northern classicism, Germanic, Nordic, something like Gunnar Asplund's, but much more dire. How fierce and wonderful those early projects were: Saint Quentin-en-Yvelines, where the school was to be a defensible city, like Roman Trier; and the later island city with its hypnotic model. Can it really be Atlantis? We wander entranced through the labyrinthine urban spaces, but what is that menacing pyramid that caps the summit? And the all too few constructed buildings: Krier's own house at Seaside, a whole acropolis in itself, climbing to the temple that crowns the upper city, looking, as at Athens, across the whole world-circle of land and water. Or the chapel at Windsor, blazing white in the sun, unimaginably thick of wall, inconceivably steep of gable: at once Parthenon and Hrothgar's Herot, the Grendel-haunted hall.

I said at the beginning that Peter retied the knot that Venturi had cut, but to confuse this by now wretched metaphor even further, I will add that Krier then seized the chariot of Gordium in Asia Minor, around whose yoke the knot was tied, and galloped off in it, a bit like Europa, all across Europe, coming at last to another homeland on the frozen Viking seas.

Clearly Leon and Peter are both formidable characters to be reckoned with, even though it has been a pure delight to have them here together. What can we say? Must we simply regard their work as embodying two of the multiple choices that the modern age ought to afford us? Or can we indeed, as Hemingway once put it, utilize them both in our Ideal City? Perhaps a town by Krier with a major building by Eisenman—New Urbanism demands no code for public buildings—might be okay. But maybe not. I cannot imagine it the other way around. The trick is that one can't invent urbanism overnight, as modernist architects, from Le Corbusier onward, following their cult of originality, have persistently tried to do, and so created several convincing versions of hell—most disastrously realized at mass scale in American redevelopment of the 1960s and the French new towns. Workable urbanism, on the other hand, has normally grown out of a long history of human use, so that the most successful and humane examples in modern times (most of them hated or ignored by old-fashioned modernists, and none of them mentioned today)—the Garden City, the City Beautiful, and the New Urbanism (badly misnamed)—have all been revivals and recombinations of traditional patterns of one kind or another (exactly what Hippodamos of Miletus did with the age-old Greek agora and the grid), in which the problems of the modern age, of mass population, the automobile, and so on, are treated *as* problems, their effects palliated, preferably healed, never celebrated or fetishized, never taken as pretexts for the creation of megalomaniacal new forms. Krier has always known this; it is the heart of his perception. It is true that Eisenman, despite his subterranean grids, has not concerned himself much with these questions up to now, but we have seen that he is beginning to do so. And he is very determined; so who can tell?

Milan Pavilions

Peter Eisenman and Leon Krier

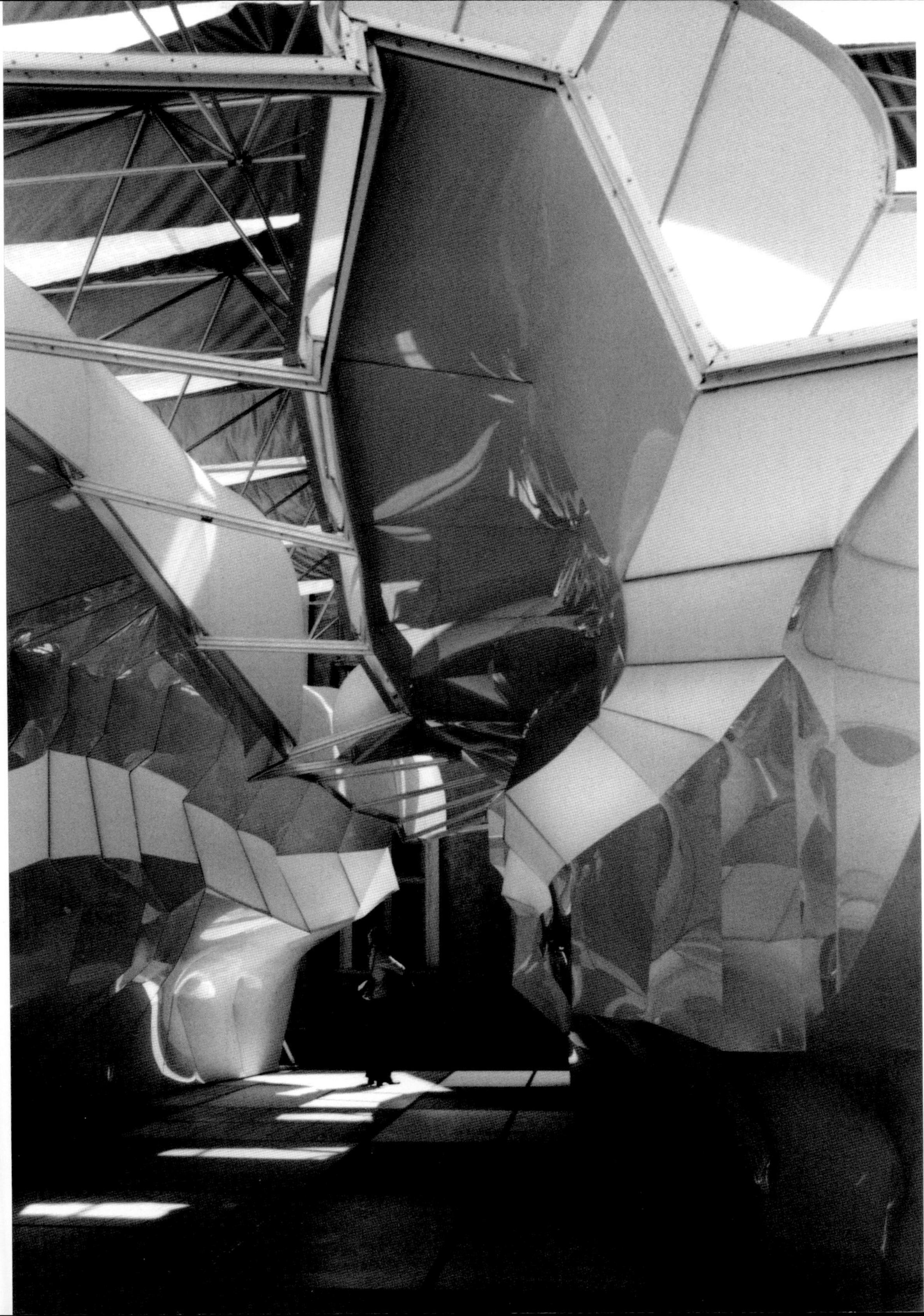

Peter Eisenman with Matteo Cainer, "The Tunnel" (temporary pavilion commissioned by *Interni* magazine and built in the streets of Milan for the Milan Furniture Fair), 2002.

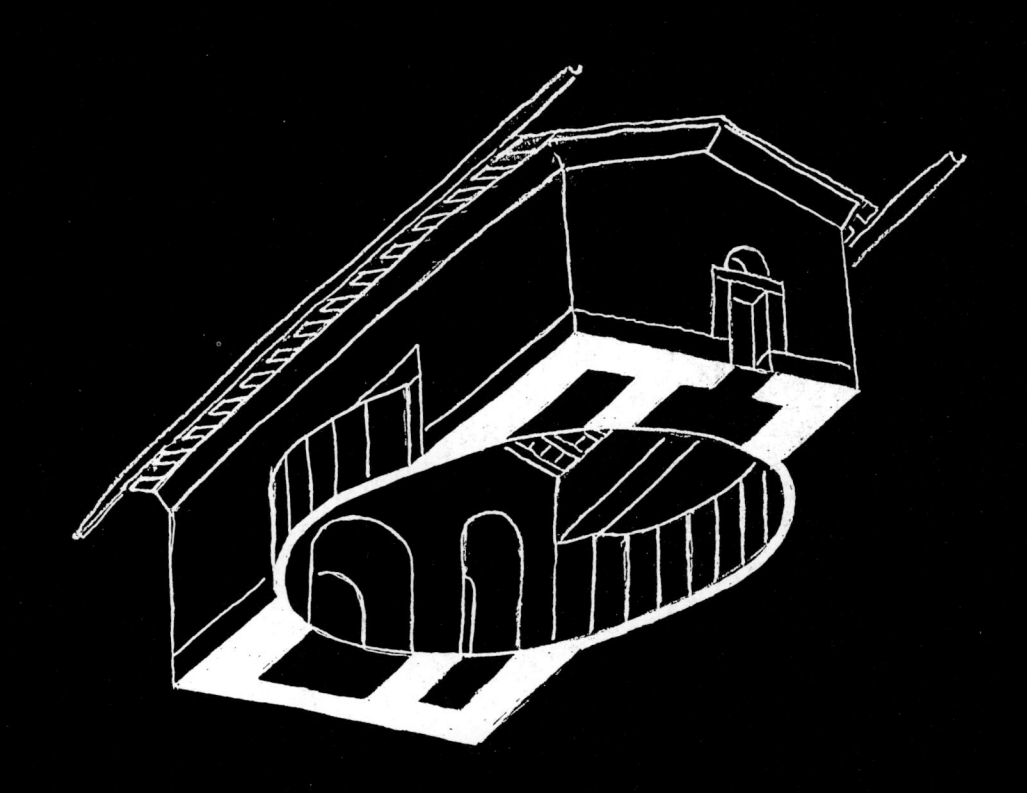

Leon Krier, "Studio for a Pianist" (temporary pavilion commissioned by *Interni* magazine and built in the streets of Milan for the Milan Furniture Fair), 2002.

STAN ALLEN is dean of the School of Architecture, Princeton University, and an architect in private practice in New York. Since 1999, he has collaborated with James Corner Field Operations on competitions and large-scale public works.

MAURICE CULOT is an architect and city planner who teaches at the Institut Français d'Architecture in Paris. His books include *Perceive, Conceive, Achieve the Sustainable City: A European Tetralogy*; *Aesthetics, Functionality, and Desirability of the Sustainable City*.

KURT W. FORSTER is a historian currently teaching at the Bauhaus University in Weimar. He is the director of the Ninth Architecture Biennale in Venice (2004).

ROGER KIMBALL is a cultural critic for the *New Criterion* and the author of several books, including *Lives of the Mind: The Use and Abuse of Intelligence from Hegel to Wodehouse*.

DEMETRI PORPHYRIOS is principal of Porphyrios Associates in London and author of *Classical Architecture*, among other volumes.

VINCENT SCULLY is the Sterling Professor Emeritus of the History of Art at Yale University. Among his books are *The Shingle Style* and *The Villas of Palladio*.

R. E. SOMOL is an assistant professor of architecture in the Department of Architecture and Urban Design at the University of California, Los Angeles, and a partner in Polari X Somol.

ANTHONY VIDLER is dean of the School of Architecture of the Cooper Union and an architectural historian. His books include *The Architectural Uncanny: Essays in the Modern Unhomely*.

SARAH WHITING is associate professor of architecture at Harvard's Graduate School of Design and a partner in the architectural firm WW in Somerville, Massachusetts.

MARK WIGLEY is dean of the School of Architecture, Planning and Preservation at Columbia University and the author of several books, including *White Walls, Designer Dresses: The Fashioning of Modern Architecture*.